Delta | Academic | Objectives

Listening and note-taking skills

Michael Thompson

DELTA PUBLISHING

DELTA Publishing
Quince Cottage
Hoe Lane
Peaslake
Surrey GU5 9SW
England

www.deltapublishing.co.uk

First published 2013

Edited by Catriona Watson-Brown
Designed by Caroline Johnston
Illustrations on pages 16 and 46 by
    Kathy Baxendale
Cover design by Peter Bushell
Printed in China by RR Donnelley

ISBN Book 978-1-905085-60-6

Author acknowledgements

I would like to thank my friends at Delta Publishing, in particular Anna Samuels, Catriona Watson-Brown and Nick Boisseau, for their kindness and their patience. Their help and feedback were invaluable. I would also like to thank my colleagues at Bocconi University and at Bicocca University for their support. And I would especially like to thank my wife Gina and my son Alex for giving me the space and love needed to complete this project.

Text acknowledgements

We are grateful to the following for permission to reproduce copyright material:
Dumb Little Man for material adapted from '8 College Courses That Will Make You Rich', by Robert (Flimjo.com), 13 May 2008, http://www.dumblittleman.com. Reproduced with permission.

Photo acknowledgements

Shutterstock (pages 8 (both), 10 (Michael C. Gray/Shutterstock.com), 21, 25 (TDC Photography/Shutterstock.com), 28 (left and centre), 33, 35, 37 (centre top, centre bottom and right), 38, 40, 42 (centre left, centre right, right), 44, 52 (all), 54, 61 (bottom), 62 (left), 63, 66 (both), 72, 82, 83, 84)
Thinkstock (pages 18 (left), 20, 37 (left), 42 (left), 51, 61 (top), 62 (right), 71 (left), 79, 80)
iStock (pages 18 (right), 28 (right), 62 (centre), 81)
Alamy (page 26)
Cartoonstock (pages 59, 64, 71 (right))

Contents

listening for production	listening for meaning	unit extension
Completing notes	Recognizing vocabulary	Courses that will make you rich
Open questions	Collocations	Woodstock
Sentence completion	Word families	Common law
Gap-fill activities	Function words	The end of the world?
Identifying key ideas	The Academic Word List	The fallacies of happiness
Working with summaries	Unfamiliar vocabulary	The history of brands

Introduction

You are already good at English. You have learned the grammar; you have acquired a lot of vocabulary; you can understand somebody when they are talking to you. Congratulations – that was not easy to do!

Now that you have developed these skills, you need a new motivation for taking your English to the next level, and one such motivation is because you want to study in English. This book forms part of the *Delta Academic Objectives* series and will help you to adapt to the challenges of studying academically in the English language.

The listenings

One key characteristic of listening in academic situations is length. Lectures and talks tend to last a long time. A key premise of this book is that if you want to get good at something, you need to practise it as much as possible. Following talks and conversations for longer periods is a skill that needs to be developed.

Throughout the book, you will meet extended listening passages that allow you to practise your listening-comprehension and note-taking skills.

This book is accompanied by three audio CDs. The complete audio transcripts for all the tracks can be found at the back of the book (pages 85–105), and these offer you the chance to explore and exploit the language used.

Aims

This book is designed for B2 and C1 users of English. B2 and C1 are levels described in the Common European Framework of Reference (CEFR). The CEFR was developed in the 1990s and is frequently used as a common standard for describing language ability.

In the CEFR, people at B2 level are considered Independent Users. If you have good B2-level listening skills, you can follow:

- speakers who are using a normal speaking rate
- speakers using a normal range of vocabulary
- speakers discussing a wide range of common topics, including topics you are not very familiar with
- extended speech when it is clearly structured and you are already familiar with the topic.

The CEFR also describes note-taking ability. If you have good B2-level note-taking skills, you can take notes on points that you think are important.

C1-level students are considered to be Proficient Users. This means that they can operate effectively in English-speaking environments. You are at a C1 level for listening and note-taking skills when you can:

- follow extended speech, even if it is not clearly structured, and even when you are not that familiar with the topic
- understand what speakers mean, even when they do not say something explicitly
- take detailed notes during a talk concerning your field of interest
- write notes that are good enough to be used by another person.

How to use this book

There are eight units in the book: six main units plus two consolidation units. All the units focus on a different topic.

At the beginning of each unit, you will find a *Topic focus* and a *Vocabulary focus*, which are designed to help you activate your knowledge of the topic. This preparation makes it easier to understand the talks and conversations you will hear.

Each of the main units also targets particular listening and note-taking skills, as well as listening strategies. The activities you will find in these sections will help you prepare for listening in real-life academic situations, as well as for situations where you need to demonstrate your level of listening comprehension. So you will also find them useful if you are preparing for one of the standardized tests which are sometimes needed in order to study in English.

Each unit ends with a *Unit extension*, which allows you to put those targeted skills into practice.

A key component of using English in academic settings is knowing academic vocabulary. For each of the main units in the book, you will find a separate exercise page targeting the vocabulary on the Academic Word List (see pages 79–84).

While there is a natural progression to the units, it is not necessary to do them in order. If you want, you can concentrate on those units most important for your field of study. It is best, though, to work through the entire unit, since the practice you get will help you acquire the targeted skills. The Consolidation units revise the skills found in the preceding three units, so it is a good idea to complete those three units before you move on to the relevant Consolidation unit.

If you are working alone or using this book for self-study, there is a full answer key at the back of the book to enable you to check your answers.

It may seem that you are being asked to do a lot. You are. You are already good at English. Getting to 'very good' takes hard work. But when you are very good, you can study effectively in English and work in English. And those are objectives that are worth doing a lot for.

Good luck.
Michael Thompson

This book is accompanied by the *Listening and note-taking skills* Teacher's Book. The Teacher's Book contains:

- step-by-step guidance for each section in this Student's Book
- **Teaching ideas**, offering variations and elaborations for many of the exercises
- **Teacher's notes**, offering further information about many of the exercises
- **Photocopiable materials** for each of the units in this Student's Book.

1 Higher education

Aims

- Listening for numbers
- Working with multiple-choice questions
- Note-taking skills: completing notes
- Recognizing vocabulary
- Using 'university' vocabulary

Topic focus

Discuss these questions in pairs.

1 How does the education system in your country work? Think about the following:
   - How many levels of school are there? How old are the students there?
   - Do students get to choose what they study?
   - If students decide to go to university, do they pay for their own education, or does the government pay?

2 In your opinion, how important is a university degree?

3 Who is more important to a university: the students or the teachers?

Vocabulary focus

1 **Here are some of the key words you will come across in this unit. Use five of them to complete the sentences below about universities in the United States.**

campus	degree	enrol	graduate	major	tuition

1 When I came here, I thought I wanted to study economics, but then I switched my _____ to biology because I realized that I'd rather work with frogs than with bankers.

2 The _____ here costs $12,000 a year, which is expensive, but a good investment when you think about how much more you can earn later on.

3 I tried to _____ in Professor Stratton's Art History class, but the list was already full.

4 It took me six years to _____ because I had to work while I was going to school.

5 I should get my Master's _____ in physics next spring, but I haven't decided yet whether I'll go on for my doctorate.

> *i* A big part of listening comprehension is understanding vocabulary in context. Before you start listening, think for a moment about the topic, and which words and phrases you are likely to hear.
> If you're not sure how to say those words or phrases in English, don't worry. Write them down in your language, then look them up.

2 🎧 1.1–1.8 **You are going to hear eight brief excerpts. Each contains one of these words or phrases linked to university. Match each word/phrase (a–h) with the excerpt you hear it in (1–8).**

a financial aid ....

b grade point average ....

c internship ....

d mid-term ....

e office hours   *Excerpt 1* ....

f prerequisite ....

g scholarship ....

h semester ....

3 🎧 1.1–1.8 **Listen again and match each of these definitions (1–7) with one of the vocabulary items in Exercise 2 (a–h).**

1 set times when teachers are in their office to help students and answer their questions about the course

2 a common period of time in a school year, often 18 weeks long

3 a general term for money given to students to help pay the cost of going to university; it can come in the form of loans, grants or even work–study programmes

4 a test taken approximately half-way through a course

5 a temporary job that helps students gain experience in their field of study

6 a class that students must take before taking a higher-level course

7 money given by an organization to help pay for the cost of education; it does not have to be repaid

> ⊸ **Going further**
> You'll notice that one of the terms in Exercise 2 did not have a definition in Exercise 3. Can you use your own words to give a definition for the missing term?

4 a Of the words and phrases in Exercises 1 and 2, which *ten* do you think are the most important to know if you want to study at a university in the United States?

b Compare your list with a partner's. Work together to prepare a single 'Top 10' list.

c Work in pairs to add ten more words and phrases that you think are important to know. Add them to your 'Top 10' list. Compare your 'Top 20' list with the rest of your class. Are there any words that appeared on every list?

1 🎧 1.9 **Listen to the first part of a conversation about the American university system and choose the best answer (a, b or c) for each of these questions.**

1 How many foreign students are studying at American colleges?
  a 150,904
  b 582,984
  c 872,964

2 What is the first step of the admissions process?
  a filling in an application
  b calculating financial aid
  c recruiting students

3 Which of the following is true about the terms *college* and *university* in the United States?
  a Americans don't make a technical distinction between the two terms.
  b *College* refers to where American students get their Master's degrees.
  c American colleges do not award degrees.

4 Which of the following is true about the term *Bachelor's degrees* in the United States?
  a They are not given to scientists.
  b It usually takes six to eight years to earn them.
  c There are a number of different Bachelor's degrees.

5 Community Colleges …
  a offer two-year programmes, rather than four.
  b award Bachelor's Degrees in fields like Engineering and Design.
  c are not valid institutions in the US.

6 Traditionally, which of the following is **not** one of the liberal arts?
  a music
  b architecture
  c geometry

7 In American colleges, core courses …
  a are required courses for most students.
  b focus on the student's primary field of study.
  c allow students to concentrate exclusively on the liberal arts.

2 🎧 **1.9 Listen again and complete these notes about Faber College.**

Number of Faber students from other countries: **1** ....
Total number of Faber students: **2** ....
Faber founded in: **3** ....
Application process:
    Step 1: Recruit students
    Step 2: Process **4** ....
    Step 3: Determine **5** ....
    Step 4: Enrol students

Major: Economics
    Courses taken:
      ● **6** ....
      ● Macro-economics
      ● **7** ....

Major: **8** ....
    Courses taken:
    ● Molecular Biology
    ● Organic Chemistry
    ● Scientific Writing

> ℹ️ After you hear something, you can usually remember the key ideas of what you've heard, but the details fade fast. Notes allow you to record the details, so that you can use them later.

3 Here are four majors offered at many American universities. Work with a partner and decide which of the courses in the box below go with each major.

  1 Engineering
  2 Business Management
  3 Media Arts
  4 Psychology

Biological Sciences	Calculus
Directing for the Screen	Dynamics of Machines
Ethics	History of the Documentary
The Science of the Mind	Management of Technology
Organizational Staffing	Principles of Accounting
Research Methods	Themes in Literature and Film

4 What other courses would you expect students with the majors in Exercise 3 to study? Can you think of two more courses for each major?

> 🔍 **Going further**
> Many big American universities offer more than 100 majors. Work in pairs. How many majors can you think of in five minutes? Many universities have their catalogues online. How many of the majors you thought of can you find?

Language focus

Large numbers **1 How would you say these numbers?**

a 42,000,305   **b** 8,500,000,000   **c** 6,700   **d** 53,166   **e** 212,301

2 🎧 **1.10 Listen and check your answers.**

> *i* If you have ever tried to remember someone's telephone number, you know how hard it can be to work with numbers with a lot of digits (the number 12 has two digits; the number 322,415 has six).
>
> Large numbers in English all have the same pattern. They are grouped into hundreds, thousands, millions, billions and trillions (quadrillion is next in line – a one with 15 zeroes – but it rarely comes up in conversation), and each group is pronounced fully. So 123 is pronounced *one hundred and twenty-three*, and 123,123 is pronounced *one hundred and twenty-three thousand, one hundred and twenty-three*.

> **⊸ Going further**
> How would you say this number?
> 123,123,123,123,123

> *i* Here are some more things to remember when you are working with large numbers:
>
> **1 *and* after the hundreds**
> British speakers and some American speakers say *and* after the 'hundreds' position (e.g. *one hundred and twenty-three*). If there is no digit in the hundreds position, they still say *and* (e.g. *two thousand and one*).
>
> **2 thousands ending with 00**
> When talking about four-digit numbers that end in 00, some speakers (especially in American English) prefer to use the word *hundred* rather than *thousand*. So for 2,500, they say *twenty-five hundred*, not *two thousand, five hundred*.
>
> **3 saying zeros**
> English offers several different ways to say *zero*. When talking about large numbers, you can say *zero* of course; but you can also say:
> ● *oh*: This is common when you are giving a number digit by digit, like a telephone number: 201 555-0102 = *two-oh-one, five-five-five, oh-one-oh-two*.
> ● *nought*: This is mostly used by British English speakers.
>
> **4 decimal points**
> If the number to the left of the decimal point is 0, it is pronounced *zero* or *oh* by American English speakers and *nought* by British English speakers. The decimal point is pronounced (as *point*). And each digit to the right of the decimal point is normally pronounced individually. So 0.35 would be pronounced *zero point three five* or *oh point three five* or *nought point three five*.
>
> **5 long-scale and short-scale numbers**
> Another challenge when working with large numbers is that there are historically two different naming systems. That would not be so bad, but the two systems use many of the same names, but use them differently. So, for example, *a billion* can refer to 1,000,000,000 (short scale) or 1,000,000,000,000 (long scale). English today mostly uses the short scale, and that is what is used in this book. But many European languages, such as French and Spanish, use the long scale, so you need to be aware of 'false friends'.

3 🎧 **1.11 Listen to six brief excerpts and tick the number you hear in each one.**

1 a 2,400,501 ☐
  b 2,055,001 ☐

2 a $50.39 million ☐
  b $53.9 million ☐

3 a 6,212 ☐
  b 6,220 ☐

4 a $3.04 billion ☐
  b $3.94 billion ☐

5 a €8,200 ☐
  b €80,200 ☐

6 a 139,596,817.6 ☐
  b 149,597,870.7 ☐

4 Work in pairs.

Student A: Turn to page 76.
Student B: Turn to page 77.

Take turns reading the excerpts out loud. Write down the numbers you hear your partner read out.

> ℹ️ There are times when people need to be precise with their numbers, but not always. When speaking generally, we often 'round off' numbers. So instead of saying 2,493, we will round off and say *almost 2,500*. Other common 'approximators' are *about, around, more or less, or so, over, roughly, under* and – of course – *approximately*.
>
> All these approximators allow you to be a bit vague, but they don't all allow you to be vague in the same way:
>
> ● With *almost* and *nearly*, the exact number has to be less than the approximate number (4,912 can be *almost 5,000*, but 5,012 cannot).
>
> ● *or so* comes after the approximate number, not before: *5,000 or so*.
>
> When the number is very large (from millions upwards), you can also use decimal points to round off. So 12,479,612 could be expressed as *almost 12.5 million*.

5 For each of these numbers, think of two ways to round them off.

1 9,106

2 29,812

3 42,817, 932, 446

4 307,108

> ⊸○ **Going further**
> Look again at the numbers you read in Exercise 4. Which ones do you think you would naturally round off? How?

Listening for production

Completing notes

> ⓘ Note-completion activities help you improve your attention to detail, which means improving your overall level of comprehension.
>
> To do well on note-completion activities, pay attention to the type of detail you need. Identifying what to listen for before you start listening will make it a lot easier for you to recognize the detail. For example, in Questions 1 and 2 of the note-completion activity you did on page 11, you needed to listen for a number. In Question 3, you needed to listen for a year, and in Question 4, you needed to listen for the direct object of the verb *process*.
>
> It's not always possible to know precisely what kind of detail you are listening for. For example, Question 3 introduces the detail with the preposition *in*, but *in* can be used to introduce places as well as years. How do you know which information is called for? In a way, you don't. So you need to remain flexible and alert to both years and places. Your judgment is another important element in your listening comprehension.

1 **Look at these notes. Work in pairs to decide what kind of details you should be listening for.**

- Harvard founded in **1** ....
- First Harvard grads received **2** .... degrees in 1642
- **3** .... Bachelor degrees awarded in US last year
- Number of US colleges/unis: **4** .... (not incl. community coll.)

Fields of study (by no. of degrees)
   Most degrees
   1 **5** .... :   327,531 degrees
   2 Social Sciences & History: **6** .... degrees
   3 Education: c. 105,000 degrees

   Fewest degrees
- **7** .... :   82 degrees
- Precision Production: 23 degrees

Avg. tuition (last year): **8** ....

Study tip
The abbreviation *c.* in the notes means 'approximately'. It comes from the Latin word *circa*. For more on abbreviations, see Unit 4.

2 🎧 1.12 **Listen to the second part of the conversation about the American university system and complete the notes in Exercise 1.**

3 🎧 1.12 **Look at these sentences from the conversation in Exercise 2. Listen again and number the sentences in the order you hear them.**

   a 'Four-year institution' does mean college or university, doesn't it? ☐

   b Thank you again for taking the time to speak with us, Dr Liebowitz. ☐

   c I really don't know the specific number. ☐

   d All right, well, away we go. ☐

   e It's quite an investment of both time and money. ☐

   f So what are all these people studying? ☐

   g Now, I understand that you'd like to share some numbers with us. ☐

   h So while American universities may not have the history of a University of Cambridge or a University of Bologna, the system has been around for more than 360 years. ☐

Listening for meaning

 • Which words do you need to know?
• Do you need to know every word you meet?
• How many words do you need to know?
No one can give you the definitive answers to those questions, but you should have enough vocabulary to operate productively in English (some studies indicate that the number of words needed is about 4,500). You should also know the topical vocabulary used in your field(s).
Students are often more comfortable reading vocabulary than listening to it. Remember, part of knowing a word is recognizing it when you see it, but it is also important to recognize the word when you hear it.

1 **1.9   Here are ten words you heard in Track 1.9. Listen again and number the words in the order you hear them.**

a areas	❏	**f** implies	❏	
b assume	❏	**g** issues	❏	
c brief	❏	**h** journals	❏	
d finally	❏	**i** policy	❏	
e founding	❏	**j** registered	❏	

 The words in Exercise 1 come from the Academic Word List (AWL). The AWL is a valuable resource for language students. It contains 570 words (word families, actually) that people studying in English often come across.

2 **1.12   Listen to Track 1.12 again and find words or phrases that mean the following.**

1 established

2 as well as

3 has existed

4 most popular

5 feel something is important

6 makes something necessary

 Take a moment before you start listening to think about the context. What vocabulary do you think you might hear? Which words and phrases do you connect with the situation? Even if you don't hear those precise words and phrases, thinking of them will help prepare your brain to recognize more vocabulary.

Going further
Recognizing a word when you hear or see it is one aspect of 'knowing' that word. Another is having a good idea of what it means. Discuss in pairs what other information you have when you 'know' a word.

3 You are on a university campus, but you are not certain that you heard correctly. Look at the situations below and, for each one, decide whether it is more likely that you heard a) or b).

1 Two students are talking about their studies.
   a I'm doing pretend.
   b I'm doing Pre-med.

2 A girl says, 'You'll be graduating in less than a year.' What was the sentence before?
   a Don't drop out now.
   b Don't pop it now.

3 A university official is introducing herself.
   a Good morning. I'm Isabelle Clancy and I'm done with students.
   b Good morning. I'm Isabelle Clancy and I'm Dean of Students.

4 A teaching assistant is ending a class.
   a And don't forget, you have to handle your assignments by next week.
   b And don't forget, you have to hand in your assignments by next week.

5 A student is describing his class schedule for the next term.
   a And then I'm taking 'Poetry in the 21st Century' as an elective.
   b And then I'm taking 'Poetry in the 21st Century' to be elected.

> ℹ️ Language learners are not the only people who have trouble distinguishing the words they hear. Native speakers also confuse things, too. (The captions in the cartoon below are famous song lyrics that have been famously misheard – can you identify them?)
> It's not always possible to be absolutely certain of what you have heard, but you can use the context to help you. If the words you think you heard don't make much sense in context, then perhaps you heard something different.

Unit extension

1 In your opinion, which university courses will help you get rich? Work together in small groups to develop a six-course 'Get rich' curriculum.

2 ⬠ 🎧 1.13 Listen to a talk on college courses that can help you get rich, then complete these notes with up to four words in each gap.

Course 1: Accounting
    Reason 1: Need to be able to read **1** _____ (tell difference between
     2 _____ and liability)
    Reason 2: Important for business owners to understand health of business
Course 2: **3** _____
    Reason 1: Need to be able to figure out what you **4** _____
    Reason 2: Helps you figure out what customers want
Course 3: Economics
    Reason 1: Teaches you **5** _____ approach
    Reason 2: Helps you figure out where **6** _____
Course 4: **7** _____
    Reason 1: Teaches you that money **8** _____ over time
    Reason 2: Need to know how money works when it's not in your hands
Course 5: Writing and Composition
    Reason 1: Need to be able to **9** _____
    Reason 2: Good writing gets you **10** _____

---

3 Use the notes in Exercise 2 to answer these questions, using your own words as far as possible. Try to write two or three sentences for each answer.

  1 How can Accounting help you get rich?

  2 How can Economics help you get rich?

  3 How can a writing course help you get rich?

4 a How many of the courses in your 'Get rich' curriculum did the speaker in Track 1.13 mention? Do you want to change any of your courses?

  b Work in small groups and prepare a three-minute presentation of your curriculum for a group of high-school students. Write a structure for your presentation that includes each course *and* two reasons why the course is included in your curriculum. Then write a brief introduction and a brief conclusion. When you are ready, present your curriculum to the class.

5 ⬠ 🎧 1.13 Here are six partial word families from the Academic Word List. Listen again and circle the form of the word you hear in each case.

  1 **a** instructor   **b** instruction   **c** instructive

  2 **a** purchasing   **b** purchaser   **c** purchased

  3 **a** identification   **b** identity   **c** identify

  4 **a** involved   **b** uninvolved   **c** involvement

  5 **a** communicable   **b** communication   **c** communicated

  6 **a** refocus   **b** focusing   **c** focused

🔍 **Going further**
Here are three more words from the Academic Word List, forms of which appear in Track 1.13. How many words can you add to each family?
1 concept   **2** invest   **3** consumption

---

2 Rock'n'Roll, Inc.

Aims
- Working with open questions
- Note-taking skills: outlines
- Working with collocations
- Using 'music industry' vocabulary

Topic focus

Discuss these questions in pairs.

1 What is your relationship with music? Think about the following:
   - How often do you listen to music?
   - What kind of music do you listen to?
   - How often do you watch music performed live?

2 What do you think about these ways of listening to music?
   a performed live
   b in the car
   c on a home stereo
   d on a portable mp3 player
   How are these experiences similar? How are they different?

3 How should musicians earn their money? Through sales of songs and albums? Through concerts?

Vocabulary focus

1 Match the words (1–7) with the definitions (a–f). There is one word that does not have a definition.

1 cover
2 gross
3 open
4 promoter
5 show
6 sold out
7 venue

a person who arranges concerts
b begin a concert for a more popular group
c place where an event takes place
d no more tickets are available
e have enough money to pay for
f earn before taxes and other expenses

Going further
Can you give a definition for the word in Exercise 1 that you did not match?

2 Complete the expressions below about the music business using the verbs in the box. You will not need one of the verbs.

book	cover	go	have	make	sell out

1 .... a venue
2 .... expenses
3 .... on tour
4 .... a concert
5 .... an experience

3 🎧 1.14 Listen to a brief introduction to the business of live music and check your answers to Exercise 2.

4 Match the sentence beginnings on the left (1–6) with their conclusions (a–f).

1 If you look at the gross, it looks like …
2 Before I sign this contract, …
3 Why do so many bands consider Madison Square Garden …
4 We lost money because we didn't sell enough tickets …
5 The show in Swansea didn't sell out, but …
6 Could you please call our promoter and find out why …

a … to even cover our costs.
b … there weren't many empty seats.
c … you made good money, but there were a lot of bills to pay.
d … I have to talk to my manager.
e … she booked us to play in Adelaide?
f … to be such an important venue?

Going further
Here is one more sentence beginning and one more sentence conclusion. Use your imagination to complete them.
1 The concert last night was OK, but the opening act …
2 … was my band's big break.

Practise your listening

1 🎧 1.15 **Short Shrift is a well-known rock band. Listen to their manager discussing the results of their 'Get Shorty' tour and choose the best answer (a, b or c) for each question.**

1 What is true about the 'Get Shorty' tour?
  a It lasted close to a year.
  b It took Short Shrift to 44 cities.
  c All the shows sold out.

2 How much did the tour gross?
  a Not quite as much as the country of Kiribati makes in a year
  b Almost $148 million
  c Just over $147.5 million, without calculating the lighting

3 What is one difference between the venues in North America and those in Europe?
  a The American venues were not suitable for concerts.
  b The American venues were smaller.
  c The American venues were each used only once.

4 Which of the following is true about attendance in Europe?
  a Roughly twice as many people saw the shows in Europe as in America.
  b More than a million people came to the show in Berlin.
  c The average attendance in Europe was over 70,000 per show.

5 The tour ended …
  a on July 10th.
  b in Belgium.
  c one month after the show in Paris.

2 🎧 1.15 **Listen again and answer these questions.**

1 Where and when did the 'Get Shorty' tour begin?
2 How many shows did the band play in the New York Metropolitan area?
3 How many people saw the shows in the New York Metropolitan area?
4 Without being exact, what was the average gross for the shows in Europe?

3 a **Here are some facts and figures about the third leg of the 'Get Shorty' tour. Work in pairs. Decide which facts and figures are important and write out a short presentation to the band. Use the audio transcript for Track 1.15 on page 88 as a model.**

Began: Toronto, Canada, Sep. 12	
Ended: Montreal, Canada, Nov. 28	
Number of shows: 28	
Sell-outs: 28	
Number of shows in NYC: 2 (both at Madison Square Garden)	
Total attendance in NYC: 37,314	
NYC gross: $3,859,828	
Total attendance: 734,712	
Average ticket price: $98.25	

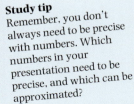

Study tip
Remember, you don't always need to be precise with numbers. Which numbers in your presentation need to be precise, and which can be approximated?

b **Take turns to give your presentation to each other.**

Language focus

Note-taking: outlines

 People take notes for many reasons. Students may take notes during a lecture so that they can study later; businesspeople may take notes during a presentation so that they can prepare a report for their boss. While the reasons for taking notes can change, the fundamental purpose of note-taking remains the same: to record information so it can be used later.

Taking good notes is an important skill to learn. Here are five keys to successful note-taking:

1 Be brief

Speakers can speak faster than writers can write. Don't try to write complete sentences – use key words or phrases, abbreviations and symbols instead.

2 Be clear

Be brief, but don't be cryptic. Remember, you need your notes for the future. If you can't understand what a symbol means or remember what 'CCR > 1st Act sgn'd x W'dstk' refers to, then your notes will not be very useful. Put those key words and phrases in context; be consistent in your use of abbreviations and symbols.

3 Identify key ideas

Writing down the key points the speaker wants to make will ensure your notes are much more effective. It will also be easier for you to organize them.

4 Pay attention to supporting information

Good speakers do not merely make a point; they offer details – examples, explanations, etc. – to make it clear *why* the idea is important.

5 Use your judgment

You do not have to write down everything the speaker says. Not every supporting detail is important. Not every supporting detail is new. If you already know it, there is no reason for you to write it down.

One common method for note-taking is to use outlines, or linear notes. With outlines, the key ideas become headings, placed on one line, and the supporting ideas are placed below, indented, like this:

Key idea
  Supporting idea 1
  Supporting idea 2

You can then add details about those supporting ideas:

Key idea
  Supporting idea 1
    Detail 1
    Detail 2

1 🎧 ▢ 1.16 **Listen to Janice Sandstrom, an entertainment lawyer, giving the first part of a talk on 'The business of concerts'. Decide which of these outline notes, A or B, better represents the key ideas in the talk.**

A

Finding work
    Supporting idea
    Supporting idea
Dealing with employers
    Supporting idea
    Supporting idea
Negotiating
    Supporting idea
    Supporting idea

B

Making a living
    Supporting idea
    Supporting idea
Recording your band
    Supporting idea
    Supporting idea
Finding work
    Supporting idea
    Supporting idea

2 🎧 ▢ 1.17 **Listen to the next part of the talk, in which Janice Sandstrom discusses the key idea of 'Finding work'. What two supporting ideas does she bring up? Complete gaps 1 and 4 in these outline notes.**

Finding work

Supporting idea: **1** ....
– club owners in area
– **2** ....
– other groups
   – opening acts?
– **3** ....

Supporting idea: **4** ....
– **5** ....
– information
   – sortable / keep track
     – what shows?
       – **6** ....
     – who?
    – clubs?
      – which nights?
      – who plays regularly?
    – **7** ....
      – how often?
        – opening acts?
    – local uni
      – how often?
      – how many bands?

3 🎧 ▢ 1.17 **Listen again and complete the remaining gaps in the notes.**

4 **Some of your friends have formed a band. With your partner, use the notes from Exercises 1–3 to write an email to your friends, giving them advice on how to enter the music business.**

Study tip
Outline notes work well when the information is well organized and structured, like a prepared talk or presentation.

Listening for production

Open questions **1** **1.17 Listen again and, in each case, choose the best *question* (a, b or c) for the answer given.**

1 A *gig*
- **a** What is a dirty term in the music business?
- **b** What is a cool way of saying 'job'?
- **c** What is another way to say 'band member'?

2 Club owners, local promoters, universities
- **a** Who talks the most about finding work?
- **b** Who sends out CVs in the music business?
- **c** Who are your potential employers?

3 Local or university newspapers
- **a** Where might you advertise the band?
- **b** Where can you find opening acts?
- **c** Where should you look for information about bands?

4 In different ways
- **a** How do you need to be able to sort information?
- **b** How can you talk to people about work?
- **c** How should you contact out-of-town bands?

> **Study tip**
> If you know something about the topic, you can anticipate the types of information you will hear.

> ℹ️ Open questions ask you to identify specific information in the listening passage. The question words will tell you which type of information to listen for.

2 Short Shrift, the band from page 20, recently went on a reunion tour. Each of these sentences is missing information about the tour. Working in pairs, write eight open questions to find out the information.

1 Short Shrift started the tour in .... before moving east to Ontario.

2 Overall, the band played .... shows in Canada.

3 The band started the tour in Canada because ....

4 It had been .... since the band was on tour.

5 The band spent some time opening for ....'s comeback tour.

6 The .... show was the only sell-out.

7 The tour grossed ....

8 The band will make a profit by ....

3 Work in pairs.

Student A: Turn to page 76.
Student B: Turn to page 78.

> ℹ️ **Tips for answering open questions**
> 1 Identify the topic of the listening passage in the instructions, where possible.
> 2 If the topic is not given, read the questions. Try to anticipate what the listening might be about.
> 3 Look at the question words so you know what kind of information to listen for.
> 4 Read the instructions carefully. Do you need to answer in complete sentences? Is there a word limit?

4 You are going to listen to a radio talk show about being a concert promoter. Discuss in pairs what kind of information the conversation might include.

5 🎧 **1.18** Listen to the conversation with a concert promoter, Isabelle Santos, and answer these questions. Do not use more than four words for any answer.

1 What is a promoter's primary job?
2 Name two things promoters are responsible for.
3 What was Isabelle's major in university?
4 Name one course that Isabelle recommends taking.
5 How long has Isabelle been a promoter?
6 Which bands normally get a guarantee?
7 What are the two common 'door split' rates mentioned by Isabelle?

> **⊸O Going further**
> Sometimes answers to open questions can be more complex. Can you write an answer to this question about Track 1.18?
> *What is a 'door split', and how does it work?*

Listening for meaning

Collocations

> ⓘ Some words are commonly found used with other words; they are known as *collocations*. Recognizing them makes it easier to follow talks and conversations, because you can treat the collocation as a single unit. In other words, instead of treating the four words in *have a good time* as four separate bits of information, you can process it as one item.

1 How many of these collocations from Track 1.18 (shown in bold) can you complete?

1 … 'promoter' is one of those **job** _____ that everybody has heard of …
2 … but maybe you're _____ **sure** what it is exactly that promoters do.
3 … promoters develop **good** _____ **relationships** with bands …
4 … the equipment you need to _____ **a show** …
5 … we make sure all those things are _____ **order**.
6 … and, well, **one** _____ **to another.**
7 But the lawyers I was working for convinced me to _____ two **courses** that have been _____ **help.**
8 … and that course _____ **the foundation.**
9 … and the _____ **thing** for me is taking the time to read the _____ **print.**
10 … so that's why it's really important to _____ **the contract** carefully …

2 🎧 **1.18** Listen again and check your answers.

3 Use six of the collocations from Exercise 1 to complete these sentences. (Be careful: you may need to change the form a little.)

1 Everything was _____ when I left, so I have no idea how everything got so messed up.

2 We prefer to use Normandy Catering at our shows because we have a _____ with them.

3 If you had read the _____ , you would have seen that we are not responsible for damage to the backstage area in the absence of security.

4 As a roadie, your _____ is basically to make sure that the band's equipment makes it from one venue to the next and is set up properly. You may also be asked to run errands for the band from time to time.

5 I started working on your performance review, but then I had to work on something urgent and, well, you know how _____ , and I never got around to finishing the review. Sorry.

6 No musician really likes practising scales, but scales _____ for you to develop good technique, and so most serious musicians appreciate them.

7 Thanks for looking after the cat while I was on tour. It was a _____ .

> **ⓘ** How do you know if something is a collocation? Collocations are determined by how often the words occur together. So the way to know whether it is a collocation or not is to look out for the words occurring together. The more you see them together, the stronger the collocation.
> Collocations are often a choice that everybody in the language community accepts. Why do bands *go on tour* instead of *make a tour*? No good reason, but they do.
> Collocations are a big part of sounding 'natural' in a language. By paying attention to which words collocate with which, you can improve both your comprehension and your communication.

4 🎧 **1.15** Listen to the discussion again, then answer these questions.

1 Which verb does the band manager use with *numbers*?

2 Which verb does the band manager use with *limelight*?

3 Which adjective does the band manager use to describe the beginning of the tour?

4 Which adjective does the band manager use with *total*?

5 Which verb does the band manager use with *stadium*?

6 Which collocation used by the band manager means the same as 'pretty good'?

Unit extension

1 🎧 **1.19** Listen to a conversation about the Woodstock Music Festival with **Dr Rodney Paltz, a contemporary historian. Which of these would *not* be a good key idea for outline notes of the conversation?**

1 The location

2 The concert

3 The concert and money

4 The Woodstock music scene

2 **Put the three remaining headings from Exercise 1 in the appropriate gap (A, B or C) in these notes.**

> **A** ....
>
> - Took place in Bethel, NY, *NOT* Woodstock (Bethel actually
>   **1** .... miles away)
> - On dairy farm owned by **2** ....
> - Only **12** .... toilets
> - No trash cans
>
> **B** ....
>
> - Full name: Woodstock Music and Art Fair: An Aquarian exposition: three days of peace and music
> - Began Friday (Aug. 15) at **9** ....
> - Richie Havens 1st act, because no one else had shown up yet
> - 31 acts played / 32 booked (**10** .... never appeared)
> - Ended Mon. not Sun. (Jimi Hendrix last act)
> - Attendance: **11** .... – .... (best guess)
>
> **C** ....
>
> - 4 partners:
>   - John **3** ....
>   - Joel Rosenman
>   - Michael **4** .... } (each received **8** $ ....
>   - Artie Kornfeld   for their shares)
>
>   Creedence Clearwater Revival – 1st act signed to play: Got **5** $ ....
>   (good money)
>   Paid tickets: **6** ....
> $1.3 million in advanced sales
> $2.6 million costs
>   4,062 people **7** ....

3 🎧 **1.19** Listen again to the conversation and complete the notes in Exercise 2 **(1–12). Do not use more than three words or numbers to complete any item. Note that the gaps are numbered in the order that the information occurs in the conversation.**

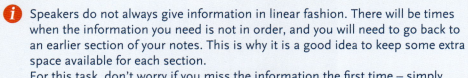

> ℹ️ Speakers do not always give information in linear fashion. There will be times when the information you need is not in order, and you will need to go back to an earlier section of your notes. This is why it is a good idea to keep some extra space available for each section.
>
> For this task, don't worry if you miss the information the first time – simply listen for it the next. Remember, the gap numbers represent the order of the information in the conversation.

4 **Answer these questions about the Woodstock Music Festival.**

1 How big was the concert site?

2 In which two newspapers did John Roberts and his partner place an ad looking for business opportunities?

3 What did Woodstock Ventures originally plan to do?

4 What was the original cost estimate for the concert?

5 When did Woodstock become a free concert?

6 How many people died at the concert?

5 **Use the notes from Exercise 2 and the answers to the questions in Exercise 4 to complete this summary about the Woodstock Music Festival with up to three words or a number for each gap.**

The Woodstock Music Festival – officially known as the 'Woodstock Music and Art Fair: An Aquarian exposition: three days of peace and music' – actually took place in
1 _____ , not Woodstock. The concert was scheduled to run from
2 _____ to 3 _____ . Disorganization, however, meant that
4 _____ (the last act) did not finish playing until Monday morning.

Woodstock was organized by four partners. Interestingly, the partnership started when two of the men – John 5 _____ and Joel Rosenman – placed an ad in the
6 _____ and 7 _____ soliciting business ideas. Originally, Woodstock Ventures (the name of the partnership) planned to build a 8 _____ in Woodstock, an artists' colony in upstate New York, but those plans eventually turned into a huge music festival.

In addition to Jimi Hendrix, 9 _____ other bands played over the three-and-a-half days. One band – 10 _____ – never made it to the concert site. While there are no firm numbers about how many people attended Woodstock, the best estimates are between 11 _____ and 12 _____ . This, in effect, meant that Woodstock was – for that weekend – New York State's third biggest city. Despite the crowds and the drug use, only three 13 _____ over the course of the weekend.

While Woodstock wound up being a free show, 14 _____ tickets were actually sold before the concert started. Still, that was not enough to cover the 15 $ _____ in expenses. Nevertheless, Woodstock eventually became both a symbol of the hippie era and a profit-making venture.

> **Going further**
>
> Can you name any of the acts that played at Woodstock? Find the list of performers online, then match 11 of them with these clues. The first one has been done for you.
>
> 1 old-time pen   Quill
> 2 sugary liquid
> 3 high temperatures, ready for a supermarket shelf
> 4 Everest
> 5 happy not to be alive
> 6 a decade later
> 7 oily musicians
> 8 foxy, with a mamma rock, a pappa rock and some baby rocks, too
> 9 flying vehicle from the US's 2nd President
> 10 veins, pores and eyes
> 11 which people

3 Whose law is it?

Aims

- Working with sentence-completion questions
- Note-taking skills: mind maps
- Working with word forms
- Talking about legal systems

Topic focus

Discuss these questions in pairs.

1 Do you agree or disagree with the statement below? Why do you agree or disagree?
   You can learn a lot about the law from watching crime shows on TV.

2 In the law, which is more important: fairness or equality?

3 Most societies base their system of law on common law, civil law or religious law (and quite often a mix of these). Match each of the above legal systems with one of these definitions:
   a system of law inspired by the Romans, focusing on statutes and codified law
   b system of law based on judges' decisions and the concept of precedent
   c system of law based on a moral sense of how people should act, influenced by the divine

4 Which system or mix of systems does your country use?

Vocabulary focus

 Another way of looking at law is to look at different types of law and which areas they cover. *Civil law*, for example, also refers to the area of law that covers how to resolve private disputes or problems between individuals.

1 These sentences describe other areas of law. Complete each of them with the most appropriate choice (a, b or c).

1 The area of law that deals with things like theft and murder is called .... law.
   a crime's   **b** criminal   **c** crimp

2 The area of law that deals with things like land and buildings is called .... law.
   a real property   **b** immobile asset   **c** land office

3 The area of law that deals with things like the quality of air and water is called .... law.
   a environmental   **b** green   **c** ambience

4 The area of law that deals with things like navigation on the high seas and shipping is called .... law.
   a dinghy   **b** maritime   **c** aquatic

5 The area of law that deals with things like being fired from a job and working conditions is called .... law.
   a employed   **b** trial   **c** labour

6 The area of law that deals with things like intellectual property and contracts is called .... law.
   a business   **b** creation   **c** patented

7 The area of law that deals with things like government power and citizens' rights is called .... law.
   a might   **b** supreme   **c** constitutional

8 The area of law that deals with things like multinational companies and treaties is called .... law.
   a country   **b** international   **c** UN

2 🎧 **1.20–1.24** **Listen to five young lawyers and match each of them with the area of law from Exercise 1 that they practise.**

Lawyer 1: ....

Lawyer 2: ....

Lawyer 3: ....

Lawyer 4: ....

Lawyer 5: ....

3 Work in pairs. Discuss which areas of law affect your life, and how.

 Don't worry if you find it confusing that the term *civil law* can refer to both an area of law and a legal system. The context will usually tell you which meaning you are talking about.
When you come across a word with multiple meanings, look for clues to figure out which meaning applies: What do the sentences before and after talk about? What other words are being used in the same context? (Do the other sentences talk about Parliament passing laws? Then the chances are that you are talking about the legal system. If the other words being used are things like *lawsuit* and *negligence*, then the chances are that you are talking about the area of law.)

Practise your listening

1 🎧 **1.25** Listen to a talk given by a high-school Social Studies teacher, and complete his notes below using the expressions from the box (a–f). There is one expression that you will not need.

> **a** Examination of Bill
> **b** Bill moves to Other House
> **c** Introduction of Bill
> **d** Nomination of Chairman
> **e** Publication of Green or White Paper
> **f** Second Reading

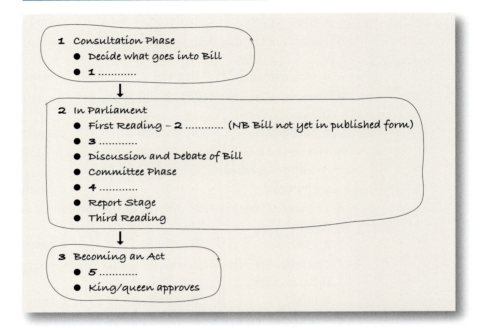

```
1  Consultation Phase
   ● Decide what goes into Bill
   ● 1 .............

2  In Parliament
   ● First Reading – 2 ............ (NB Bill not yet in published form)
   ● 3 ............
   ● Discussion and Debate of Bill
   ● Committee Phase
   ● 4 ............
   ● Report Stage
   ● Third Reading

3  Becoming an Act
   ● 5 ............
   ● King/queen approves
```

2 🎧 **1.25** Listen to the talk again and complete these sentences.

1 In a Civics course, you study what it means to _____ .
2 A Bill is basically a _____ for a new law.
3 The public has an opportunity to _____ and make comments about the Bill.
4 Parliament votes on the Bill during the _____ .
5 '_____' is the term used when the king or queen makes the Bill an Act of Parliament.
6 The last time a British monarch _____ was in 1708.

> ℹ️ Look again at the sentences in Exercise 2 and compare them with the audio transcript on page 91. Did you notice how some important words changed form?

3 How are laws passed in your country? Discuss in pairs and compare the procedure with the procedure in the UK.

> 🔍 **Going further**
> Learning how laws are passed is an important element in most Civics courses. Go online in pairs and learn how a Bill becomes law in the United States. Then prepare a short presentation to give to the rest of your class.

Language focus

Note-taking: mind maps

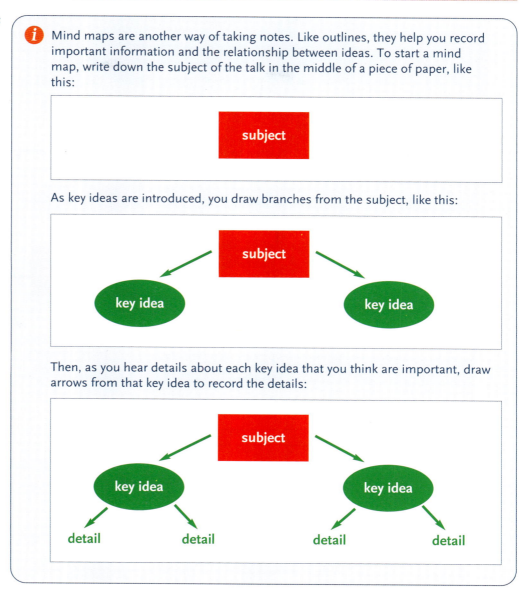

i Mind maps are another way of taking notes. Like outlines, they help you record important information and the relationship between ideas. To start a mind map, write down the subject of the talk in the middle of a piece of paper, like this:

subject

As key ideas are introduced, you draw branches from the subject, like this:

subject
key idea
key idea

Then, as you hear details about each key idea that you think are important, draw arrows from that key idea to record the details:

subject
key idea
key idea
detail
detail
detail
detail

1 🎧 **1.26** Listen to part of a lecture about legal systems in the world, and choose which mind map (A or B) better represents the lecture.

A

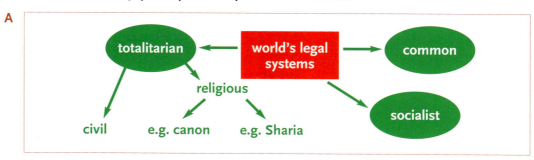

totalitarian ← world's legal systems → common
religious
socialist
civil   e.g. canon   e.g. Sharia

B

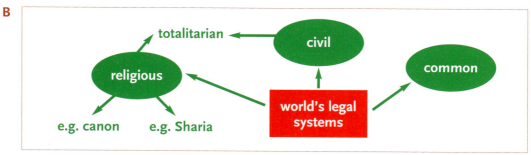

totalitarian ← civil
religious
common
e.g. canon   e.g. Sharia   world's legal systems

2 🎧 1.27 **Listen to the next part of the lecture and complete this mind map.**

four parts (all with **6** ....)

Justinian Codes ← **fundamentals of civil law** → Laws come from **1** ....

Civil, aka **4** .... law

(Common law, otoh, comes from **3** ....)

2 '................. body'

Issued in **5** .... AD

not right

codified

🔍 **Going further**
Use this mind map to write two paragraphs about Sealand, a 'micronation' located off the coast of the United Kingdom.

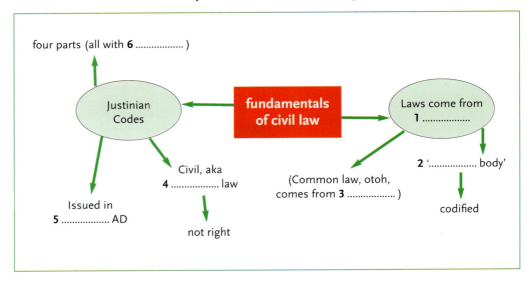

1968
ruling by UK judge
Sealand outside UK territorial waters

1967
founded by Roy Bates

history

1975
constitution
passports

1999

Sealand

2012
Roy Bates died
son Michael = 'Prince Regent'

sea fort ← North Sea ← location

10km from coast
international waters

HM Fort Roughs
old gun platform
WWII

Listening for production

Sentence completion **1** 🎧 **1.28 Listen to a talk about international law and complete these sentences, using one word or a number in each gap.**

1 The number of countries in the world ranges from 193 to _____ , depending on the source.

2 The speaker uses the word '_____' to talk about territory.

3 One characteristic that sovereign states share is _____ control over the territory.

4 The speaker compares the world's sovereign states to members of a _____ .

> ℹ️ Sentence-completion activities are a way to evaluate your understanding of the details in a listening passage. In that way, they are similar to note-completion activities. Sentence-completion activities offer a complication, though: the sentence you complete has to be grammatically correct. So you need to both identify the missing information *and* fit it into the structure of the sentence.
>
> **Tips for doing well on sentence-completion activities**
> 1 Read the entire sentence first and think about what type of information is missing.
> 2 Look carefully at the sentence structure and think about what type of words can be used in the gap (nouns, verbs, adjectives, etc.).
> 3 Look carefully at the words that surround the gap in the sentence. Words like articles and prepositions indicate what type of word is needed, and often limit which words are possible.
> 4 Be prepared to change the form of the word. It is common to hear the word in one form in the passage (as a verb, for example) but need another form (a noun, say) to grammatically complete the sentence.

Study tip
Read the instructions carefully when you are doing a sentence-completion activity: they often limit the number of words you can use. (Exercise 1 limits you to one word or a number; Exercise 3 does not give you a specific limit.)

2 Look at these incomplete sentences about Track 1.28. In pairs, discuss what type of information is missing, what type of words are needed, and whether there are any other clues to the missing information.

1 According to _____ , there are 193 sovereign states.

2 One problem with defining a nation is determining how many _____ people have to have to be considered one nation.

3 One characteristic that sovereign states share is that the territory and the population of the state do _____ on an outside power.

4 There is no _____ of what a sovereign state is.

3 🎧 **1.28 Listen again and complete the sentences in Exercise 2.**

4 Work in pairs. You are going to read further extracts from the talk on international law (Track 1.28).

Student A: Turn to page 77.
Student B: Turn to page 78.

> 🔍 **Going further**
> Work in pairs to answer this question in no more than **two** sentences:
> *How is the constitutive school of sovereignty different from the declarative school?*

Listening for meaning

> ℹ️ Word families are an essential part of expanding your vocabulary and your comprehension. Knowing the different forms used with nouns, verbs, adjectives and adverbs can help you figure out how a word is being used.
> Here are four things to think about when working with word families:
> - What is the base word? The base word is usually the starting point for understanding the meaning.
> - What grammatical forms – such as plurals and past tenses – does the word take?
> - What suffixes can be used? Suffixes – found at the end of the word – usually tell us what role the word has in the sentence (noun, verb, adjective, adverb).
> - What prefixes can be used? Prefixes – found at the beginning of the word – usually work on the meaning of the word.

1 **Complete each of these sentences with the correct form of the word in brackets. (The words in brackets all come from the talk in Track 1.28.)**

1 How would you ___*define*___ the word 'sovereign'? (*definition*)

2 You can count on Molly. She's one of the most _____ people I know. (*depends*)

3 I thought it was a very _____ presentation. There was nothing new in it at all. (*origin*)

4 I know how much you like pizza, Mr President, but I cannot stress enough that _____ all the pizzerias in the country is a terrible idea. Government and pizza-making do not mix. (*nation*)

5 The case was thrown out of court because it was discovered that the Coast Guard stopped the boat outside _____ waters. (*territory*)

6 _____ always promise you a lot before they're elected, but then afterwards they don't always deliver. (*politically*)

2 **Some of the word families in the Academic Word List – which you met in Unit 1 – have more than 10 members. Work in pairs and write down as many forms as you can for these word families.**

1 constitutional   2 create   3 interpretation   4 liberal   5 normal

3 🎧 **1.29 You are going to hear eight sentences, all of which contain words from the Academic Word List. Complete these sentences so that they have a similar meaning to the sentences you hear.**

1 The committee is trying ___*to codify*___ the rules for becoming a member.

2 If we want to be taken seriously, we need _____ the decision.

3 Unless we keep working to meet the criteria outlined in the Montevideo Convention, we will _____ our independence.

4 There is no way you can _____ another Home Office study on why prisoners want to get out of jail.

5 _____ to gamble in your country?

6 In the USA, Congress has _____ power.

7 The Treaty of St Germain is _____ in this situation.

8 It is always an important event when a new sovereign state is _____ .

Study tip
Remember, sentence-completion questions often ask you to change the form of the words, without changing the meaning of what you heard.

Unit extension

1 **Match the beginnings of the sentences about common law (1–4) with their conclusions (a–d).**

1 Despite the fact that Hong Kong was returned to China in 1997, …

2 Criminal law is usually based on …

3 The English common law and statutes that were in effect in 1603 …

4 Even though Canada is a common-law country, …

a … Quebec continues to use civil law for provincial matters.

b … it continues to use common law.

c … statutes rather than precedent.

d … are usually treated as law in the United States.

2 🎧 **1.30** **Listen to a conversation about common law between a student and a professor, and complete this mind map.**

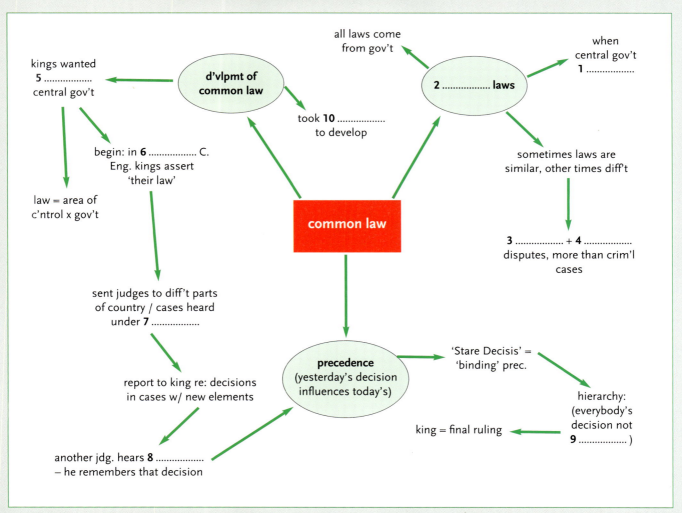

kings wanted **5** .... central gov't

d'vlpmt of common law

all laws come from gov't

2 .... laws

when central gov't **1** ....

took **10** .... to develop

begin: in **6** .... C. Eng. kings assert 'their law'

law = area of c'ntrol x gov't

sent judges to diff't parts of country / cases heard under **7** ....

common law

sometimes laws are similar, other times diff't

3 .... + **4** .... disputes, more than crim'l cases

report to king re: decisions in cases w/ new elements

precedence (yesterday's decision influences today's)

'Stare Decisis' = 'binding' prec.

hierarchy: (everybody's decision not **9** ....)

king = final ruling

another jdg. hears **8** .... – he remembers that decision

3 Use the mind map from Exercise 2 to complete these sentences with up to four words or a number in each gap.

1 Local laws can be found where _____ .

2 Common law began to develop in England in _____ .

3 _____ was important to English kings because law is an area of authority for a government.

4 Upon their return, the judges would give a report to the king about the cases they had heard, particularly _____ .

5 A _____ is a decision made yesterday that influences which decision will be made today.

6 Building up the system of common law took _____ years.

4 ⌒ 1.30 Listen again to the conversation. Each of these words is used in the conversation, *in a different form*. Write down the form that you hear.

1 study   *student*

2 difficult

3 confusion

4 local

5 explain

6 conclude

7 like

8 correction

9 reason

5 You heard a number of 'verb + noun' collocations in Track 1.30. Do you remember which verbs are used with these nouns?

1 _____ a lecture

2 _____ a question

3 _____ a problem

4 _____ the law

5 _____ your authority

6 _____ a case

7 _____ a report

8 _____ a precedent

> ⊸O **Going further**
>
> If you look again at the mind map on page 35, you will see that a number of abbreviations have been used. (You will read more about abbreviations and note-taking in Unit 4.) Without looking at the audio transcript, can you say what each of the abbreviations stands for?

Consolidation 1

Topic focus

Discuss these questions in pairs.

1 How many types of media can you think of? Which of them do you use regularly?

2 Will newspapers still exist 25 years from now? Television networks? Radio stations? How will you get your news and entertainment in the future?

3 Here are some words and phrases connected to media. Work in pairs and decide if they are associated with TV or newspapers (or both).

circulation   digital   satellite   print

viewing fees

TV   journalist   **newspapers**

spot   antenna

ad revenues   subscribe

appliance   classified ad

⚲ Going further
What other vocabulary can you think of to talk about TV and newspapers? In pairs, list as many words as you can in three minutes.

Vocabulary focus

1 🎧 2.1 **Listen to an extract about the traditional mass media and tick the words you hear.**

daily	☐	dominant	☐	half	☐	illegal	☐
kept	☐	longer	☐	onto	☐	revelling	☐
should	☐	stations	☐	struggle	☐	view	☐

2 🎧 2.1 **Listen again and answer these questions about collocations used in the recording.**

1 Which verb is used to complete the phrase _____ *a role*?

2 Which verb is used to complete the phrase _____ *even*?

3 Which preposition is used with the noun *paywalls*?

4 Which noun is used to complete the compound noun _____ *providers*?

5 Which preposition is used with the noun *pressure*?

3 **Work in pairs to use each of the phrases in Exercise 2 in a sentence.**

Practise your listening

1 🎧 2.2 **Listen to a talk by Richard Wexler, a private equity investor, on the future of the newspaper industry and choose the most appropriate answer (a, b or c) for each question.**

1 How is *readership* defined for newspapers?
   a advertisements plus number of individual subscribers
   b news-stand sales only
   c news-stand sales plus subscriptions

2 From an investor's point of view, readership is a complication because …
   a it represents a newspaper company's primary product, and yet it doesn't normally turn a profit.
   b the system that newspapers have for increasing their number of readers no longer works.
   c newspapers cannot guarantee that their product will always be delivered to their readers.

3 How many daily newspapers were there a decade ago?
  a roughly 1,500
  b just over 1,400
  c 4,500, more or less

4 Which of these is an example of a classified ad?
  a an advertisement from a car manufacturer
  b an advertisement placed by the owner for a house
  c an advertisement about a sale at a computer shop

5 Last quarter, how much ad revenue did online newspapers generate?
  a about the same as print newspapers
  b around $260 million
  c a bit over $27.5 million

6 What observation does Mr Wexler make about paywalls?
  a Early evidence is that they do not generate revenue.
  b Consumers have not yet accepted the idea.
  c They will only work if journalists change their attitude.

2 🎧 2.2 **Listen to the talk again and complete these sentences with up to four words or a number in each gap.**

  1 In addition to readership, newspapers' revenues come from _____ .
  2 Last year, there were _____ daily newspapers.
  3 _____ is one way to measure readership.
  4 For the past four years, print-ad revenues _____ .
  5 If the paywall model of online newspapers is going to work, then there will have to be _____ .

3 **How do you pronounce these numbers?**
  a 16.6   **b** 23   **c** 27.5 million   **d** 48,600,000
  e 56,182,635   **f** 69,125,573   **g** 37.85 billion

4 **Look at these notes about the talk. In pairs, decide what the abbreviations are short for.**

> **1** circulation c. 10 yrs ago: _____
> **2** circulation lst yr: approx. _____
> **3** decline in ad. rev. (%): _____
> **4** ad. revenues lst yr ($): _____
> **5** online ad. rev. lst qrtr: approx. ($) _____
> **6** % of people willing to pay x content: approx. _____

5 🎧 2.2 **Listen again and match the numbers from Exercise 3 (a–g) with the notes in Exercise 4 (1–6).**

6 🎧 2.2 **You did not use one of the numbers from Exercise 3 to complete the notes in Exercise 5. Can you say what it refers to? Listen again to check your answer.**

⊸O **Going further**
Use your own words to answer this question:
Why doesn't Richard Wexler think it is a good idea to invest in newspapers?

Unit extension

1 **🎧 2.3 Listen to a brief presentation about mass media and answer these questions.**

1 When was the term *mass media* first used?

2 What is the main characteristic of mass media?

3 What two reasons does the speaker give for the expansion of mass media in the 20th century?

4 What does the number *1.9 billion* refer to?

5 What is *unbundling*?

2 **Use your answers to the questions in Exercise 1 to complete these outline notes.**

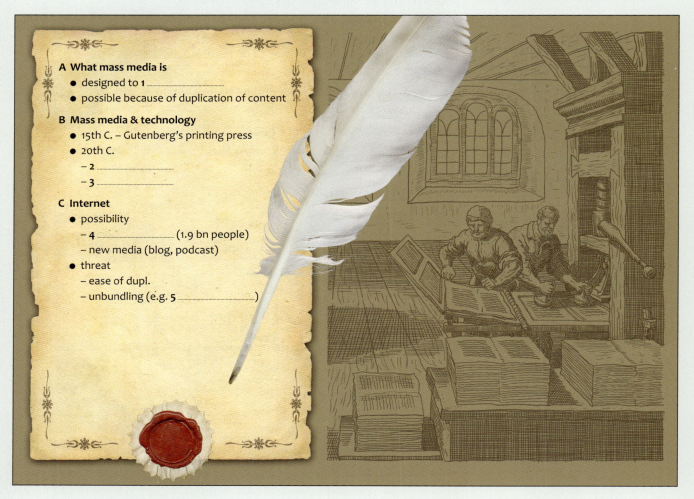

A What mass media is
- designed to 1 ....
- possible because of duplication of content

B Mass media & technology
- 15th C. – Gutenberg's printing press
- 20th C.
  - 2 ....
  - 3 ....

C Internet
- possibility
  - 4 .... (1.9 bn people)
  - new media (blog, podcast)
- threat
  - ease of dupl.
  - unbundling (e.g. 5 ....)

3 **🎧 2.4 Listen to a conversation about television in the 21st century and write appropriate questions for these answers.**

1 'Appliance' and 'content'

2 Even if the Internet provides 'television' content, we will still think of the content as television.

3 $900,000

4 Because they are lazy.

5 700 million people

4 Complete these excerpts from Track 2.4 using the correct form of the word in brackets.

1 Dr Haskell, you were saying before that, as a television historian, you don't think TV is _____ a thing of the past. (*necessity*)

2 What I mean by that is that the amazing growth of the Internet as an entertainment medium and a news-_____ medium … (*gather*)

3 Well, it's always interesting to see how language shades our _____ of something out there in the world. (*concept*)

4 … I don't think that one fact will change our _____ to television. (*relate*)

5 … if the BBC decides to develop a new drama series, the _____ works out to be … (*project*)

6 Each of these is _____ for television in the 21st century. (*problem*)

7 You make it sound like the future of television rests on people's _____ . (*lazy*)

8 You know, back in 1968, there was a _____ election in the United States … (*president*)

5 🎧 **2.4 Listen again and check your answers.**

6 🎧 **2.4 Work in pairs. Listen to the conversation again and use a mind map to take notes about these topics.**

Student A
- costs of producing television content
- how broadcasters generate revenue
- reasons for optimism

Student B
- television and the Internet
- ad revenues
- cultural aspects of television.

7 Recently, Marsha Gille Eathain became head of Bognorian Broadcasting Services (BBS), the biggest television network in the Democratic Republic of Bognor. She has asked employees at BBS to email her whenever they have ideas about how to make BBS more successful in the future.

You and your partner work for BBS. Use your notes from Exercise 6 (as well as the information in Track 2.4) to write an email to Ms Gille Eathain explaining what you think BBS should do to be successful in the 21st century. Try to write at least 200 words.

To: Marsha Gille Eathain
Cc:
Re: The future of broadcasting

4 Death by universe

- Working with gap-fill questions
- Working with abbreviations
- Working with function words
- Talking about disasters

Topic focus

1 Work in pairs. Do you agree or disagree with these statements?

1 Space exploration is the key to human survival.

2 The biggest threat to human existence is humans, not nature.

3 If scientists determined that the world was going to end in ten days, I would want to know.

2 In pairs, rank these disasters. You will need to decide *how* to rank them first.

alien attack	asteroid strike	bio-tech disaster
climate change	computer overlords	drug-resistant bacteria
earthquake	epidemic	extinction
landslide	nuclear accident	supernova

3 Add the disasters from Exercise 2 to this mind map.

⚲ Going further

Work in pairs and see how many other disasters you can add to each category in the next three minutes.

Vocabulary focus

1 **Match the words and phrases in the ovals with the word they are used with: *space* or *disaster*.**

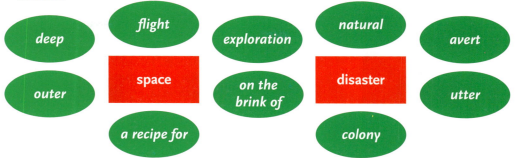

deep flight exploration natural avert

outer **space** on the brink of **disaster** utter

a recipe for colony

2 **Use six of the combinations from Exercise 1 to write six sentences.**

3 **Do this quick quiz about some of the vocabulary in this unit.**

1 If your financial advisor tells you that a certain investment is a *black hole*, she probably means that you will …
a continue to invest more money in it every year.
b put your money in, but never get it out.
c have to wait a very long time to see a profit.
d profit greatly because it invests in space-age technology.

2 Which of the following is **not** a synonym for *wipe out*?
a destroy
b kill off
c end up
d annihilate

3 'We are ready to turn on the *particle accelerator*.' Can you explain what a particle accelerator does, using only THREE words? (Hint: one of the words is *it*.)

4 If you cannot resist a person's charm, then you find that person's charm …
a non-resistant.
b irresistible.
c resistantless.
d unresisted.

5 What's the missing word in this sentence?
The dodo _____ extinct in the late 17th century because of hunting and animals introduced into its habitat by humans.

6 Monty has given you three cards. The cards are face down, so you cannot see what they are, but you know there are two black cards and one red card. How would you complete this sentence?
If Monty asks you to choose the red card, you have a _____ chance of picking the right card.

ⓘ Death by … what? The phrase *death by X* was originally used by professionals to indicate the cause or means of death. A doctor might conclude that a person had died from *death by gunshot*; a judge might sentence the murderer to *death by hanging*.

Over time, popular culture has borrowed the phrase and applied it to things that don't really kill you but which imply a surfeit or abundance of something. *Death by chocolate* can be used to promote your new dessert, *Death by PowerPoint* to explain why you don't like meetings.

Language professionals call these phrases 'snowclones'. Other examples include *The mother of all X*, which began with Saddam Hussein to refer to the 1991 Gulf War, and now includes such 'mothers' as *the mother of all bailouts* to refer to the 2008 financial crisis and *the mother of all traffic jams* to refer to just about every traffic jam anybody has ever been in.

⚲ Going further

Look online for two other common snowclones. Can you explain to your partner how they are used? Can you use them yourself over the next few days?

Practise your listening

1 🎧 **2.6 Listen to a talk given about ways the world could end and complete this table.**

event	damage	probability	preventable?
solar flares	collapsed power grids / depletion of ozone layer	(of dying) 0%	**1** _____
asteroid impact	depends on size	(of dying) **2** one in _____	yes
supernova	destruction of ozone layer / radiation	(of it happening) **3** one in _____	no
gamma-ray burst	Earth set **4** _____	(of it happening) one in 14 million	**5** _____
6 _____	Earth destroyed	(of it happening) one in a **7** _____	no

2 🎧 **2.6 Listen again to find words and phrases that match these meanings.**

1 well-known
2 adjective form of *galaxy*
3 system for delivering electricity to people
4 finish coming down from the sky
5 a notice that something bad could happen
6 fill up with too much
7 pulled by force, like a liquid
8 probability

3 🎧 **2.7 Listen to the continuation of the talk and complete the gaps in the audio transcript with the words and numbers you hear.**

Now, on to Martians and other aliens. Of course, we can't say **1** _____ it is that aliens are a threat to our existence, given that there isn't **2** _____ evidence that aliens even exist. What I can say is that in 1995, we only knew of three exoplanets – **3** _____ I mean planets outside our solar system. But at the last count, we were **4** _____ , and I'm sure that number will continue to rise.
But since we don't know for certain that aliens are out there, there's no way for us to **5** _____ . So the answer to the question of 'What are my chances of dying in an alien attack?' is a big '**6** _____ '. And I'll leave it to you to decide whether that's better or worse than one in a trillion. On the other hand, we could prevent an alien attack **7** _____ conditions, so that's something in our favour.

> ℹ️ How fast was that? Gap-fill activities are normally recorded at slower speeds than regular listening passages, to give you time to focus on the precise words used.
> Track 2.7 was recorded at a speed of roughly 130 words per minute (wpm). The average speed for the listenings in this book is 150–165 wpm, which is a natural rate for talks and conversations.

Language focus

Abbreviations

 Speed is essential when you are taking notes: people can speak faster than you can write, and they are not going to wait for you. Abbreviations are an important part of writing information down quickly.
Experienced note-takers usually develop their own system of abbreviations. (After all, notes tend to be for personal use.) Nevertheless, there are some common methods of abbreviating information in notes, including using initials.

Initials
Few people would take the trouble to write out *the United Nations* in their notes: *the UN* would be sufficient. Similarly, most people would recognize that *NYC* means *New York City*. What the initials mean sometimes depends on the context. For example, *CIA* can refer to spies (the Central Intelligence Agency) or cooks (the Culinary Institute of America). When you use initials in your notes, make sure the context is clear.

Latin abbreviations
Many people use abbreviations for Latin expressions in their notes (even if they don't always know that the abbreviation comes from Latin). The abbreviation *etc.*, for example, comes from the Latin *et cetera*, and means that there are other items in the list; *cf.* comes from *conferre* and is used to compare one thing to another.

1 **What do these common initials stand for?**

1 AKA

2 BBC

3 EU

4 FAQ

5 MBA

6 OTOH

2 **Match each of these common Latin abbreviations (1–5) with its use (a–e).**

1	c.	a	to indicate something important
2	e.g.	b	to explain more fully
3	i.e.	c	to give an approximation
4	NB	d	to indicate the subject matter
5	Re	e	to give an example

 Shortened words
Most people would recognize that *Dept* means *Department* or that *wrd* means *word*. There are three common methods for shortening words (which are often used in combination):
1 Use the first syllable(s) of the word.
2 Drop the final letters of the word.
3 Leave out the vowels (and some consonants) of the word.
Sometimes we can get too enthusiastic about shortening our words. When you are using less common abbreviations, it is a good idea to write the word out in full the first time you use it in your notes, so you have a clear idea of which word the abbreviation refers to.
It also sometimes helps to use an apostrophe to show where the missing letters were.
Full stops are generally used at the end of abbreviations if the last letter of the abbreviation is different to the last letter of the full word.

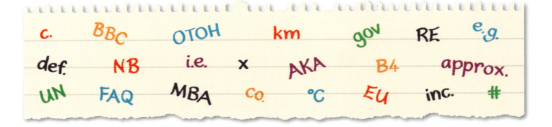

3 Do you know the common abbreviations for these words?

1 captain   2 example   3 government   4 incorporated
5 kilometre   6 systematic

4 **2.8 Listen to ten brief statements and write down the initials and abbreviations that you hear.**

> **Going further**
> Not all of the initials and abbreviations you just heard are common. How many of them do you know?

> **ⓘ Symbols**
> People often use symbols when taking notes, for example: ↓ for *go down*; ← for *caused by* or *is the result of*; = for *equals* or *is the same as*. Letters and numbers, too, can be used for symbols: *B2B* is a common abbreviation for *business to business*. Three common categories of symbols are:
> 1 numbers and trends
> 2 relationships
> 3 certain words.

Study tip
Remember that you have to be able to understand what you have written. Abbreviations are a personal choice, but be consistent in how you use them. You don't want to have to figure out what you meant later on.

5 What do these common symbols mean?

1 B4   2 ???   3 #   4 3x   5 →   6 !

6 **2.9 Listen to an extract from a talk on epidemics. Six of these notes refer to things that are said during the talk. Identify the two notes which do *not* represent information mentioned in the extract.**

1   20m kld by Sp. flu (1918)

2   Blk Dth = bub. plague (c. ⅓ Eurpns kld)

3   gms almst alwys strgr than hums

4   rsks t'dy: AIDS, Ebola, etc.

5   2mny antibtcs → resistance (e.g. cholera + tuberc.)

6   mst serious thrt = cholera + tuberc.

7   c. 30 difft staph bact. (most hrmless, some v. dang.) / bcming more resist.

8   c. 12,000 yrs ago mny west hem. mammals extnct (cause = disease???)

7 One way to use notes effectively is to turn them into complete sentences soon after you take them. This helps you process the information, and makes it easier to study the notes later on. Work in pairs to turn the six notes taken from Track 2.9 in Exercise 6 into complete sentences.

Listening for production

Gap-fill activities

 Gap-fill activities are a common way to practise (and test) your ability to concentrate on the words that the speakers use. They are also a common way to practise (and test) your ability to process English grammar (which verb tense was used, which word form, etc.).

The key to doing well on gap-fill activities is to be accurate.
1 Read the text before the first listening, so you know where to pay particular attention.
2 Anticipate what kind of words are missing: should you be listening for a finite verb, for example, or a comparative adjective? English sentence structure is full of clues – use them to your advantage.
3 After the listening, go back and make sure your answers make grammatical sense. Remember that you are completing sentences.
4 Understanding meaning is not enough. You need to identify which words were used.

1 **Look at the first part of the audio transcript from Track 2.9 and answer the questions below about the gaps.**

Of all the possible disasters for humankind, one of **1** _____ comes from Mother Nature: a global epidemic. The last time we had a true global epidemic was in 1918, when a Spanish Flu epidemic killed at least 20 million people. In **2** _____ , the Black Death, which was a bubonic-plague epidemic, is estimated **3** _____ one-third of the European population. Humans have been battling germs for as long as we've been on the planet, and it's clear that sometimes the germs get **4** _____ . People tend to think that epidemics are a thing of the past, but people still die of the bubonic plague today; AIDS is still an **5** _____ , and quote-unquote newer diseases like Ebola have the potential to explode out of their contained areas.

1 Gap 1 will contain a …
  a superlative adjective.
  b relative clause.
  c number.

2 We know that gap 2 contains a time because …
  a no other type of information can go in the gap.
  b the signal phrase *in addition* would not make sense in this sentence.
  c the sentence already includes information about 'where'.

3 We know that one of the words missing in gap 3 is …
  a the infinitive marker *to*.
  b a modal auxiliary.
  c an *–ing* form.

4 Which of these statements about gap 4 is true?
  a The final word cannot be a noun.
  b None of the words can be an adjective.
  c At least one of the words will be the object of the verb *get*.

5 What characteristics must the word(s) in gap 5 have?

Study tip
Don't worry if you found it a little more difficult to focus on the precise words in this activity. Remember that it was recorded at natural speed.

2 🎧 2.9 **Now listen again and complete the text in Exercise 1 with the words you hear.**

3 Look at this text from a student presentation about the Spanish Flu epidemic. Work in pairs to analyze what kind of information is missing in the gaps, and what the words might be. There are up to four words missing in each gap.

World War I began in August 1914, and by the time it ended in November 1918, **1** _____ people had been killed by the war. By contrast, an estimated 20 million plus people died during the Spanish Flu epidemic, which began in March of 1918 and **2** _____ 1920.

It is difficult to overstate the effects of the epidemic. **3** _____ is estimated to have been as high as 3% of all humans. **4** _____ worse by the fact that adults aged 20 to 40 were particularly susceptible to the disease. This is unusual, because the people **5** _____ dying from the flu are normally the very young and the very old. For obvious reasons, the **6** _____ in World War I affected the same age group. The combination of war and epidemic **7** _____ dramatically. In the United States, it fell by more than ten years.

The Spanish Flu does **8** _____ the past. In 2005, researchers managed to determine the **9** _____ , and in 2007, monkeys were infected with the re-created flu. Let's hope that humans are better prepared to face the Spanish Flu **10** _____ a comeback.

4 🎧 **2.10** Listen to the presentation and complete the gaps with the words and numbers you hear.

5 This passage giving advice on how to avoid getting the flu during the next epidemic is 130 words long. Practise reading it out loud until you can read it in 60 seconds. (You will probably need to read it a few times before you can do this.)

> The Spanish Flu epidemic was the worst flu outbreak of the 20th century, but it was not the only one. And while no one can say when the next flu outbreak will come, experts can say that it is a question of 'when it comes', not 'if it comes'.
>
> When it comes, there are things you can do to keep yourself and your family safe. The most important thing to do is to limit your contact with other people. If you are ill and have a fever, you will need to stay home for at least 24 hours after the fever has gone. To avoid becoming ill, you should stay away from public spaces like theatres and sports stadiums. And remember to wash your hands as often as you can.

6 If you needed to prepare a gap-fill exercise for a lesson, which words would you take out of the text in Exercise 5? Discuss in pairs.

7 a Find (or write) a brief passage about a threat to human existence (the passage should not be more than 250 words long). Create ten gaps in it, each containing one to three words or numbers, and give the gap-fill activity to your partner for them to try and complete the gaps.

b Read the passage out loud to your partner twice, then correct their answers. Try to read at the same speed you used for Exercise 5.

Listening for meaning

Function words

1 Here are the 15 most-used words in English. What class of words are they (e.g. nouns, verbs, articles, etc.)?

Most-used English words

1 the	6 in	11 for
2 be	7 to	12 I
3 of	8 have	13 that
4 and	9 it	14 you
5 a	10 to	15 he

Source: British National Corpus

> **Study tip**
> Perhaps you noticed that the word *to* is listed twice. The *to* in number 7 is the *to* used with infinitive verbs (technically called the 'infinitive marker'). The preposition *to* is at number 10.

2 Here are the word classes for the next 15 most-used words in English. What do the abbreviations mean?

16 prep	21 adv	26 poss
17 prep	22 det	27 det
18 v	23 conj	28 pron
19 prep	24 prep	29 conj
20 prep	25 pron	30 det (or pron)

3 Work in pairs to think of what the 15 words in Exercise 2 might be.

> ℹ️ • There are many ways to categorize words in English. One way is to make a distinction between 'content' words and 'function' words.
>   Nouns, verbs, adjectives and most adverbs are content words. The category 'function words' includes articles, auxiliaries, conjunctions (and other linking words), prepositions, pronouns and question words. In general, function words are grammatical words that help give structure to the sentence; content words express more meaning (though, of course a number of function words have meaning).
> • Most of the words on the Academic Word List are content words, but there are some function words, too, e.g.
>
> | | | | | |
> |---|---|---|---|---|
> | *albeit* | *despite* | *furthermore* | *hence* | *likewise* |
> | *nevertheless* | *nonetheless* | *notwithstanding* | *plus* | *somewhat* |
> | *thereby* | *via* | *whereby* | *whereas* | |
>
> Can you use each of these function words in a sentence?
> • The distinction between content words and function words is important in listening. English pronunciation depends on stress. In a spoken English sentence, the stressed syllables occur at regular intervals, more or less. That means that some syllables (and words) in a spoken English sentence will not be stressed. Function words are often unstressed in spoken English.
> • Function words *are* stressed when they are important to the meaning of the sentence. (For example, if the previous sentence were spoken, the auxiliary verb *are* would be stressed.)

4 Work in pairs to identify the function words in this extract from a talk about black holes.

But what would happen if our solar system came into contact with a black hole? Few scientists take the chances of this happening very seriously, but scientists do estimate that there are about ten million dead stars in the Milky Way alone, and dead stars are the building blocks of black holes.

5 How do you think the two sentences in Exercise 4 will be pronounced? Are there any function words that you think will be stressed?

6 🎧 **2.11** Listen and mark the function words in Exercise 4 that are stressed.

> ℹ️ Unstressed words (and syllables) are harder to understand. They are pronounced more quickly and less clearly. One reason function words can so often be unstressed is that the grammar and the structure of the sentence limit what the words can be.

7 Complete the next part of the talk below with the function words in the box. There are three words that you will not need.

a	but	do	every	have	in	may	some
some	than	that	there	those	to	won't	

Not **1** _____ dead star becomes **2** _____ black hole, of course, **3** _____ **4** _____ of them **5** _____ ; in particular, **6** _____ stars with more **7** _____ 20 times the mass of our Sun do. **8** _____ scientists estimate **9** _____ **10** _____ **11** _____ be hundreds of black holes **12** _____ our galaxy.

8 🎧 **2.12** Listen and check your answers.

9 Here is the next part of the talk. Some of the function words have been removed. Work in pairs to determine what the words could be. (Be careful: some of the gaps may need more than one word.)

Most should be in orbit around the centre **1** _____ galaxy, and in fact, current theory holds that the galaxy **2** _____ is orbiting a massive black hole. But space is a violent place, and some of the smaller black holes could be flung **3** _____ centre. And the theory also holds that once these black holes are no longer orbiting the centre of the galaxy, they can roam **4** _____ the galaxy, a bit like asteroids in our solar system.

5 _____ the size of our galaxy, the likelihood that the Earth will actually run into **6** _____ rogue black holes, as they're called, is quite small. But a black hole doesn't have to hit Earth to make life here very uncomfortable. **7** _____ comes close – and close astronomically speaking is about a billion miles – then its gravitational pull could change the planet's orbit, **8** _____ lead to extreme changes in temperature, and the end of human life on Earth.

10 🎧 **2.13** Listen and complete the gaps in Exercise 9 with the words you hear.

> 🔍 **Going further**
> Go through the brief passage you found or wrote for Exercise 7 on page 48 and identify the function words. What class of words are they? Which function words did you stress when you read the passage out loud?

Unit extension

1 🎧 2.14 **Listen to an interview with Dr Alma Nassar, head of the Earth Sciences Department at Faber College. Work in pairs to determine what the abbreviations in these notes about the interview mean.**

- Dr Nassar tchs **1** _____ / AKA **2** _____ 101
- **3** _____ % all spcies now extnct
- x 75% of E., people dead w/in **4** _____ w/out spcl equip.

Ecosystem collapse
- E'sytm = rlt'ships b'twn **5** _____ in a gvn area
- Liv'g in time of mass extnct.
  # spcies extnct in r'frst each yr = up 2 **6** _____
- trpcl r'frst collap. cld → no air x humns

Mgntc. pole revers.: (N↔S)
Solar radiat. (s'brnd to death)
lst revers. **7** _____ ago

Part. acc.
Loc: Genv. + L. Isl. **8** _____ of NYC
Could create:
a. **9** _____
b. **10** _____ AKA strangelet

2 🎧 2.14 **Listen again and complete the notes in Exercise 1.**

🔍 **Going further**
Which abbreviations did you use to complete the notes in Exercise 1? Compare your abbreviations with a partner's.

ℹ️ The Large Hadron Collider (LHC) in Geneva began operations in 2008. CERN, the organization that runs the LHC, offers detailed information on its website about strangelets, black holes and other potential 'dangers'. Check it out.

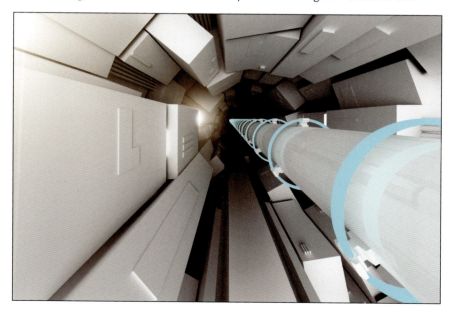

5 Happiness is ...

Aims

- Identifying key ideas
- Working with organizing signals
- Working with the Academic Word List
- Talking about happiness

Topic focus

Discuss these questions in pairs.

1 When you are tired or stressed out, what makes you happier: staying by yourself or going out with your friends?

2 How important is money to happiness?

3 At work, which three of these factors are the most important to your happiness?
   a high salary
   b praise from your boss
   c hard-working colleagues
   d flexible working hours
   e career potential
   f independence
   g pleasant working environment

4 How do you define happiness?

Vocabulary focus

1 🎧 🔊 2.15 **These 12 words and phrases all appear in this unit. Listen to 11 definitions and match each of them (1–11) with one of these words or phrases (a–l).**

a adversity ☐		**g** approach ☐
b blame ☐		**h** dissatisfied ☐
c insight ☐		**i** no way ☒
d outcome ☐		**j** pleasure ☐
e self-esteem ☐		**k** standing ☐
f strike out ☐		**l** turn out ☐

2 **Write a definition for the word in Exercise 1 for which you did not hear a definition.**

> ⓘ A phrase like *no way* is known as an 'emphasizer'; in other words, you use it to make what you are saying stronger. For example, *There is no way the board will accept the proposal* is a stronger way of saying *The board will not accept the proposal.*
> Other common emphasizers are *really* (e.g. *I really like having a full English breakfast at the weekend*) and *absolutely* (e.g. *I was absolutely gobsmacked when I saw some Americans putting ketchup on their haggis*).
> Emphasizers are an important signal about how the speaker sees the information.

3 **Complete these sentences using words and phrases from Exercise 1. You may need to change the form of some of them.**

1 What was the _____ of the job interview? Did you get the position?

2 There is _____ that Luke can eat 50 hard-boiled eggs in an hour. It's impossible.

3 The growing _____ felt by the workers is a direct result of the fact that they have not been given a raise in over two years.

4 The president has a lot less _____ with the Board of Directors these days because the company is losing a lot of money.

5 'It's all John's fault that we lost the contract.'
'I disagree. John did everything he possibly could. He's _____ in this situation.'

6 I don't have as much negotiating experience as you do, but are you sure that rejecting every offer they make is the right _____ ?

7 Thank you, Lara, for your _____ presentation on how the Russian market works. The information you've given us will help us make St Petersburg our most successful franchise yet.

8 In the end, things didn't _____ so well: Marcia lost her job, and Marshall lost his marbles.

> 🔍 **Going further**
> Which three of the words or phrases from Exercise 1 would you like to use better? Can you write your own sentence for each?

Practise your listening

1 🎧 **2.16 Listen to a talk about lawyers and depression, then work in pairs to decide which three of the following are key ideas of the talk.**

a Lawyers' tendency to be more pessimistic than most professionals

b The performance of law students

c The effects of a negative thinking style

d How Martin Seligman has influenced psychology

e Ways to become less pessimistic

2 a 🎧 **2.16 Work in pairs. Listen again and complete the notes.**

Student A: Turn to page 77.
Student B: Turn to page 78.

b **Work together and use your notes from Exercise 2a to complete this summary.**

Studies have shown that lawyers are more pessimistic than most other workers. Twenty years ago, research carried out by William Eaton looked at **1** _____ different occupations, and found that lawyers are **2** _____ times more likely to suffer from depression than other workers. Another study at the University of **3** _____ showed that while optimistic students generally do better in school than pessimistic students, in law school the opposite is true, with pessimists outperforming the optimists.

Dr Martin Seligman, one of the founders of the **4** _____ Movement, says that one explanation for why pessimists make better law students could be that pessimists are **5** _____ .

This characteristic is important because lawyers are trained to identify what could go wrong. As Dr Seligman notes, however, after spending the day anticipating **6** _____ , it is a characteristic that is difficult to turn off.

Another possible contributor to the high depression rate is that lawyers do not enjoy **7** _____ , which leads to low self-esteem. In a poll, even **8** _____ were rated as being more honest than lawyers.

According to Dr Seligman, it is possible for lawyers to develop a more optimistic outlook. One key is to recognize that pessimism does have some advantages. For one thing, pessimists have **9** _____ grasp on reality. They are also better at **10** _____ . Another key is developing a better work–life balance, allowing friends and family to counterbalance the negativity of the profession. Finally, Dr Seligman recommends learning the technique of 'disputing'.

🔍 Going further

Perhaps you have heard that English does not allow 'double negatives'. You should not say, for example, *We don't need no badges.* Rather you should say *We don't need any badges.*

But there are times when you can use a double negative. For example, you can use *not* + a negative adjective. In this case, the two negatives cancel each other out. So, in effect, *It's not unusual* means that it is (fairly) usual.

There are two examples of double negatives in Track 2.16. (There is also one in the notes for Exercise 2a.) Can you identify them?

Language focus

 In general, speakers want you to understand them and follow what they are saying. One way they help you is by using signals to give you information about how all the information they are talking about is organized. If you listen carefully – and if they are thoughtful speakers – you will hear signals that tell you how one bit of information relates to another and which information is key information. Speakers will also tell you about the structure of their talk: what the topics are, how the information is divided into sections, and when they are moving from one section to another. Then, when they are finished, they will give you a brief summary of what you have heard. Signals make following what speakers are saying much easier.

Connection signals

Words and phrases such as *but*, *due to*, *so* and *be that as it may* point to the connection of one bit of information to another. For example, *I like swimming,* **but** *I don't like going to swimming pools* tells us that the speaker sees a contrast between the information about swimming and the information about swimming pools. Common connection signals talk about causes, results, contrasts and concessions (when you say that one bit of information is true, but unimportant compared to the other piece of information).

1 **Add these words and phrases to the correct column of the table below. Can you think of at least one other word or phrase used for each category?**

albeit   ~~be that as it may~~   because of   ~~but~~   consequently
~~due to~~   however   on the other hand   owing to   regardless of
since   still   ~~so~~   therefore   the result is   whereas

cause	concession	contrast	result
due to	be that as it may	but	so

 Concession
Concession plays an important role in lectures and presentations. (Saying that information A is true, but that it doesn't change the point in information B is one of the classic strategies of making an argument. It dates back at least as far as Aristotle.)
Remember that the point being conceded is not the important point. Look at this statement by a lecturer:

It is not easy to measure happiness. Nevertheless, the study of happiness is becoming more and more established in the fields of both Psychology and Economics.

The lecturer is focusing on the fact that happiness is becoming established and not on the fact that it is not easy to measure.

Text organization signals

Lecturers and presenters usually organize their material before they start speaking, and even if they don't, they will impose some sort of organization while they are speaking. These are some important uses of text organization signals:

- Adding
- Summarizing the talk
- Reaching a logical conclusion
- Introducing the topic
- Beginning a new section
- Ending a section
- Listing
- Returning to a topic

2 Match each of these groups of words and phrases (1–8) with the category of organization they are signalling from the box at the bottom of page 55.

1 and so / thus / and that means …

2 I'd like to speak about … / Today we're going to look at … / Let me start by …

3 First of all … , then … , next … / Firstly … , secondly … , thirdly … / The first is … , the second is … , the next is …

4 Let's move on to … / Turning to … / The next thing we need to look at is …

5 Let's recap, shall we? / To sum up, … / So, what have we discussed?

6 Another thing … / In addition, … / Furthermore, …

7 Getting back to … / As I was saying, … / Let's return to the question at hand.

8 So much for … / Finally, … / Before we move on, does anybody have any questions?

3 Work in pairs and add at least one more signal to each group in Exercise 2.

4 2.17–2.24 **Listen to the eight short excerpts and answer these questions.**

1 In excerpt 1, why doesn't the company have the money to give raises this year?

2 In excerpt 2, what point does the speaker concede about André?

3 In excerpt 3, what can we expect other Criminology professors to require of their students?

4 In excerpt 4, what is the difference in the way imports and exports are calculated?

5 In excerpt 5, what effect will the law of diminishing returns have on computer size?

6 In excerpt 6, what point does Speaker 2 concede?

7 In excerpt 7, why are the SAT scores of Faber College students higher today than they were five years ago?

8 In excerpt 8, the speaker uses two signals. What are they, and to which of the eight categories in the box on page 55 do they belong?

5 2.17–2.24 **Listen to the excerpts again and tick the signals that you hear.**

although	☐	and so	☐	be that as it may	☐
in spite of	☐	nevertheless	☐	on the other hand	☐
owing to	☐	regardless	☐	still	☐
the result of that is	☐	while	☐		

> **Going further**
> Work in pairs to write short excerpts that use the two signals you did not hear in Exercise 5 plus two additional signals of your choice. Perform your excerpts for the rest of the class.

> *i* In addition to navigating meaning, we need to navigate structure when we use signal phrases. Signal phrases can be conjunctions, prepositions or adverbs.

6 Rewrite these sentences using the signal phrases given in brackets.

1 Lawyers are trained to think about risk. As a result, they tend to look for the worst-case scenario. (*so*)

2 Antonio has a pessimistic personality. Nevertheless, he is known as 'the happy lawyer'. (*in spite of*)

3 Optimists generally do better at university than pessimists, but this is not true of law students. (*whereas*)

Listing for production

Identifying key ideas 1 🎧 2.25 **Listen to the introduction to a talk and answer these questions.**

    1 What will the rest of the talk be about?

    2 Which signal does the speaker use to let you know what the talk will be about?

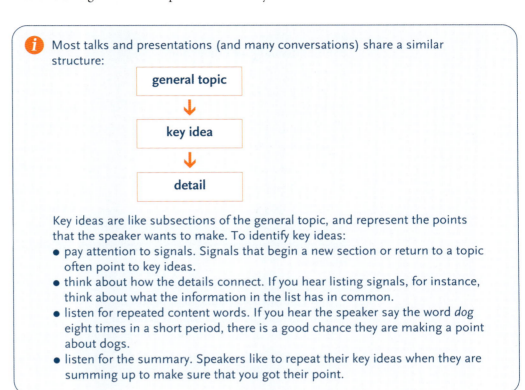

i Most talks and presentations (and many conversations) share a similar structure:

> general topic
> ↓
> key idea
> ↓
> detail

Key ideas are like subsections of the general topic, and represent the points that the speaker wants to make. To identify key ideas:

- pay attention to signals. Signals that begin a new section or return to a topic often point to key ideas.
- think about how the details connect. If you hear listing signals, for instance, think about what the information in the list has in common.
- listen for repeated content words. If you hear the speaker say the word *dog* eight times in a short period, there is a good chance they are making a point about dogs.
- listen for the summary. Speakers like to repeat their key ideas when they are summing up to make sure that you got their point.

2 🎧 2.26 **Listen to the next part of the talk. What is the key idea in this section? Discuss in pairs how you identified the key idea.**

3 What will the key idea of the next section most likely be?

4 🎧 2.27 **Listen to the next part of the talk and complete this mind map. Put each key idea in a circle and add one piece of information about the key idea below it.**

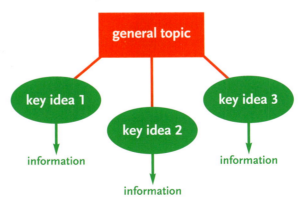

i As you might imagine, *so* is one of the most common words in English (it ranks in the top 50 words). In spoken English, *so* is often used to signal a change of topic or a movement from one section to another, and it is often used together with other signals. If you hear *so*, you should pay attention; it probably means that the speaker is moving on to something new.

5 Match the beginnings of the sentences about learned optimism (1–7) with their conclusions (a–g).

1 People often confuse optimism with positive thinking, despite the fact that …

2 Since some days are worse than the day before, …

3 Optimism, on the other hand, …

4 While optimism is a strategy to explain why something has gone right, …

5 The topic of the talk is 'learned optimism' and so …

6 The three Ps, in short, …

7 Pessimists normally feel the fault is theirs, whereas …

a … positive thinking's focus on daily improvement can lead to an inaccurate world view.

b … its real value is to explain why something has gone wrong.

c … we can conclude that optimism is a strategy that can be learned.

d … are the key areas where optimists and pessimists have different explanatory styles.

e … optimists look to someone else.

f … they are two different things.

g … is a strategy that focuses on explaining what happens to us.

6 Read these situations and, for each one, decide whether A or B is your more likely reaction.

1 You invite some friends for dinner. As they are leaving, they compliment you on the roasted brussels sprouts you prepared.
 A My greengrocer sells good vegetables.
 B I put a lot of effort into preparing those brussels sprouts.

2 A radio station has a contest in which you have to answer a question about 1970s pop music. You call the station and win the contest.
 A It was my lucky day because my call is the one that got through.
 B Isn't it great that I can still remember Gloria Gaynor, Blue Oyster Cult and all those other great artists?

3 You apply for a university programme in Australia, but you do not get in.
 A The other candidates must really be smart.
 B I guess I'm not as intelligent as I thought I was.

4 Your cousin asks you for advice on how to study English effectively.
 A He knows I give good advice.
 B He knows I'm using this book.

5 You lose all your money in the stock market.
 A I shouldn't have bought those stocks.
 B I was foolish to think I could be a successful investor.

6 You complete your first 15-kilometre foot race.
 A If I keep training, I'll be able to run a 20-kilometre race.
 B I succeeded because I always work hard to do what I say I'm going to do.

7 It is 1918, but you don't get the Spanish Flu.
 A It's a good thing not many people in my village got the flu.
 B I was very careful about washing my hands and staying away from public places.

8 You're too tired to go out with your friends.
 A I haven't been sleeping well this week.
 B My life is so hectic that I can never relax.

7 Discuss your answers in pairs. Which answer in each case is more optimistic?

> **⊸O Going further**
> The speaker in Tracks 2.26 and 2.27 discussed the 'three Ps'. Can you match each of the questions in Exercise 6 to one of the three Ps?

Listening for meaning

The Academic Word List

> **ⓘ** Averil Coxhead, who compiled the Academic Word List (AWL), looked at 3.5 million words, from a large variety of sources, to identify the words most useful to students. Just as importantly, she looked at a wide variety of materials from close to 30 different subject areas.
>
> Why is the AWL so valuable? Because the words on the list are words that you will frequently need if you are studying or working professionally, and because the words on the list are words that you will need regardless of the area you are studying or working in.
>
> The 570 word families of the AWL are organized around the head word for each family. In addition to the head word, the word family also includes other frequently used forms of the word.

1 🎧 2.16 Listen again and tick the items from the Academic Word List that you hear.

accurate ☐ aspect ☐ convinced ☐ evaluating ☐ factors ☐
issues ☐ outcome ☐ proceedings ☐ research ☐ scenario ☐

2 🎧 2.16 You did not hear these five head words from the Academic Word List in Track 2.16, but you did hear a member of their word families. Listen again and write down the word that was used. The words are listed in the order in which they occur.

1 occupy   2 apparent   3 achieve   4 anticipate   5 specific

> **Study tip**
> The AWL is a very practical list that is worth studying. For example, did you know that so far in this unit, you have heard a word from the AWL over 100 times?

3 Complete this table with the correct forms of the words from the Academic Word List.

verb	noun (thing)	noun (person)	adjective
analyze	analysis	1 _____	analytical
benefit	2 _____	beneficiary	3 _____
conform	4 _____	5 _____	conforming
6 _____	minimalization	minimalist	7 _____
respond	8 _____	9 _____	10 _____

> **🔍 Going further**
> Which three words in the table would you like to use better? Write a sentence for each.

'All the nutritional benefits of regular worms without the hassle of having to get up early.'

www.CartoonStock.com

5 Happiness is ...   59

4 Do this crossword puzzle. All the answers are Academic Word List words that you have heard in this unit.

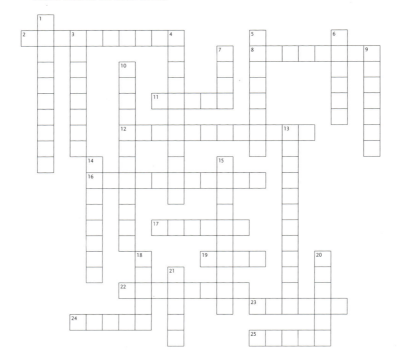

Across
- **2** limit or restriction
- **8** proof
- **11** ultimate
- **12** planning for the future, maybe even looking forward to
- **16** jobs
- **17** give a guarantee, remove doubts
- **19** chances
- **22** precision or reflection of reality
- **23** matters, questions
- **24** how people see you
- **25** table, diagram

Down
- **1** why you want to do something
- **3** what might happen, perhaps in part of a play
- **4** not modern
- **5** good things that come
- **6** without peer
- **7** football objective
- **9** products that leave your country
- **10** suddenly, impressively (like a serious actor)
- **13** even so
- **14** opposite
- **15** say the opposite is true
- **18** something that happens again and again, like a wheel going round
- **20** opposite of *accept*
- **21** what someone says directly

⊸O Going further

You may not know the words in the crossword puzzle as well as you would like. One effective way of learning vocabulary is to use flash cards.

To prepare a flash card
1. Cut some heavy paper into rectangles (three rectangles per sheet of A4 paper would be good).
2. On one side of the paper, write the word you want to learn better.
3. On the other side, write down the information you want to know:
   - its definition
   - its pronunciation
   - its translation into your language
   - important collocations
   - its word class (noun, verb, preposition, etc.)
   - how it is used in a sentence

   etc.
4. When you have a collection of flash cards (at least 20 or 25), test yourself. Keep testing yourself until you know the word automatically, and then remove it from the collection (but remember to review it once in a while).

These days, there are a number of computer programs that let you prepare flash cards on your computer.

Unit extension

1 🎧 **2.28 Listen and number these sentences in the order you hear them.**

a Sixty-nine to one. ☐

b Let's just say that our instinctive approach when it comes to statistics is an obstacle to our happiness. ☐

c You see, Tolstoy famously observed that unhappy families are each unhappy in their own way. ☐

d Well, the odds are important if we want to determine which things we should be doing in order to increase our happiness. ☐

e Nevertheless, it turns out that there are a number of common mistakes we make that make our worlds less happy than they could be. ☐

f And yet, when scientists began to look at the question of happiness scientifically, research showed that while there may not be many absolute keys to happiness, there are, indeed, common key factors that lead to happiness. ☐ 1

g How should we calculate value? ☐

h I'm afraid not; you're more likely to win the lottery. ☐

i And the nice lady there informs you that the gallery owner and the artist have settled their differences, and that the painting now costs 1,100 euros. ☐

j The first reason is that we're not particularly good at calculating probability. ☐

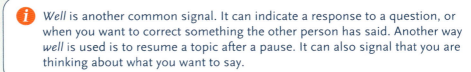

> ⓘ *Well* is another common signal. It can indicate a response to a question, or when you want to correct something the other person has said. Another way *well* is used is to resume a topic after a pause. It can also signal that you are thinking about what you want to say.

2 **The instructions for listening activities in this book usually tell you what the listening is about. Rewrite the instructions for Exercise 1, completing this sentence:**

Listen to a radio roundtable on …

3 **The conversation in Track 2.28 is organized around two key ideas. What are they?**

4 🎧 **2.28 Listen to the conversation again and answer these questions.**

1 What are the odds of winning the lottery?

2 Dr Park and Dr Diaz use the information about odds to support which key idea?

3 Which word does Dr Park use to describe our instinctive approach to statistics?

4 Complete this sentence:
We should calculate value by looking at what else we …

5 What point does Dr Diaz want to make with her example of the art gallery?

5 a **Drs Park and Diaz have identified two other common mistakes we make about our happiness. Decide in pairs what you think these other two mistakes might be.**

b **In pairs, use your notes and answers from this page to prepare a one-page handout about the four mistakes we make concerning happiness. The handout can be for either new students at a university or new employees at a business.**

6 Brand new

- Working with summaries
- Signals that manage information
- Working with unfamiliar vocabulary
- Using marketing vocabulary

Topic focus

Discuss these questions in pairs.

1 In your country, which brands have a positive image? Which ones have a negative image? Describe what some of those images are.

2 How do brands affect what you buy? Do you pay attention to brands when you buy clothes? Food? Computer products? Music?

3 What do you think *your* brand image is? If you could rebrand yourself, what would you change?

Vocabulary focus

1 These adjectives can all be used to describe brands. Work in pairs and complete the table below, according to whether each adjective has a positive or a negative connotation for you. How many other adjectives can you add?

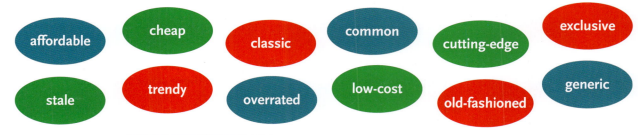

affordable   cheap   classic   common   cutting-edge   exclusive

stale   trendy   overrated   low-cost   old-fashioned   generic

positive	negative

2 🎧 **3.1** Write down the 12 marketing terms you hear.

3 Use ten of the 12 terms you wrote in Exercise 2 to complete these sentences. Don't change the form of the word. Where a sentence has two gaps, the same term is used in both gaps.

1 If we want to sell more of our frozen yoghurt drink, we need to convince .... to buy more of it.

2 Harvard's .... is the Latin word *Veritas*. My university's .... is the Latin phrase *Canis pensum meum comedit*.

3 Roger, this is the third month in a row you haven't reached your .... target. If you don't sell at least 25 insurance policies next month, we're going to have to let you go.

4 .... placement is when a company gets a film or television programme to use its .... in a scene.

5 A good marketing .... is run with military-like precision.

6 We think that the .... of this new mirror will be seven years.

7 We don't need a .... because we have a monopoly.

8 We need to consider .... our chain of restaurants because the number-one association people make with our name is 'health-code violation'.

9 When we have a tight deadline, no one is more focused and no one works harder than Sally, despite the fact that she projects this .... of just being interested in having a good time.

10 We have decided to .... our new computer game next autumn, in time for Christmas.

> 🔍 **Going further**
> In Exercise 3, you did not use two of the terms from Exercise 2. Can you use them to come up with two sentences of your own?

Practise your listening

1 🎧 **3.2** Listen to a conversation about rebranding and complete these sentences with up to two words in each gap.

1 The website for the rat campaign is www.............................. .

2 On the website, you can buy merchandise such as ...., thongs, ... and cookies.

3 The EU motto 'Unity in diversity' was written by ....

4 The justification for uniting Europe used to be avoiding another ...., but that reason is no longer relevant.

5 There are different reasons for deciding to rebrand, including .... with the past, mergers and acquisitions, and signalling a new direction.

6 Before deciding to rebrand, companies need to remember that the old brand ....

2 Which of these is *not* a key idea raised in the conversation in Exercise 1?

1 How rebranding works

2 Why organizations rebrand

3 Rebranding after a merger

4 The effectiveness of rebranding

3 **3.2 Six of the sentences in this summary contain incorrect information. Listen to the conversation again, then work in pairs to identify and correct the six sentences.**

Rebranding occurs for a number of reasons. One fundamental reason is that the past is not the present, and the needs of the brand's consumers may have changed, or the brand may be seen as old-fashioned. Another reason is globalization. A famous example of this is what happened with Marathon and Snickers chocolate bars. Both brands represented the same bar, but in the interests of global advertising, the parent company decided to rebrand Snickers as Marathon. Other reasons for rebranding are combating negative connotations, mergers and acquisitions, and signalling a new direction.

Rebranding can mean anything from changing the brand's logo to changing the brand's name. British American Tobacco, for example, changed its name to Altria because it did not want to be connected with tobacco any more.

In the case of the European Union, a decision to rebrand was taken in 1993, because it was clear that European citizens did not relate to the idea of preventing a new World War II. Unfortunately, the new motto – 'Unity in diversity' – was declared unconstitutional.

Another case of rebranding is the case of the common rat. A few years ago, a campaign was launched to rebrand the common rat 'The Great Pointed Archer'. A website – which even sold merchandise – was set up, and advertisements were produced. It was discovered that an advertising agency had set up the campaign as a hoax.

Before rebranding, it is important to remember that the old brand no longer has value. The rebranding has to increase value, or it will not be successful.

---

i
- The information in the summary is not in the same order as the information in the listening.
- When you summarize, don't include your opinions and observations (they usually come after the summary) – 'repackage' the information to suit your style.

---

4 Look at these four candidates for rebranding. Working in small groups, choose one and prepare a brief oral presentation that explains a) what its current brand image is, and b) how you think it should be rebranded. (Should it get a new name? A new motto or slogan? A new advertising campaign?) Don't forget to include reasons for your choices.

- professional football
- the United Nations
- the nuclear power industry
- spinach

'It's broccoli, dear.'
'I say it's spinach, and I say "No way!".'

www.CartoonStock.com

Language focus

 Speakers often have to convey a lot of information, particularly when they are speaking in a more structured situation. During talks, lectures and presentations, for example, they use signals to indicate what the context of the information is.
- *A lot of popular foods have been rebranded.* **For example**, *the Chilean sea bass used to be known as the somewhat less appetizing Patagonian toothfish.*
- *I never pay attention to brands.* **In fact**, *almost everything I buy is generic.*

1 In each section of this table, there is one word or phrase that does not belong. Can you identify it?

1 Giving examples For example, … For what it's worth, … For instance, …	**5 Focusing or specifying the information** Specifically, … Or rather … In particular, …
2 Expanding on an idea If I could draw your attention to … In fact, … Besides, …	**6 Reminding the audience of earlier information** As for … As we've already seen, … As I was saying, …
3 Rephrasing the information In other words, … That is, … By the way, …	**7 Referring to information that is not new or surprising to the audience** After all, … Whereas … It goes without saying that …
4 Generalizing On the whole, … After all, … In general, …	**8 Emphasizing important information** What's interesting is … And this is really the key … To cut a long story short, …

Going further

Add one other word or phrase to each category in Exercise 1.

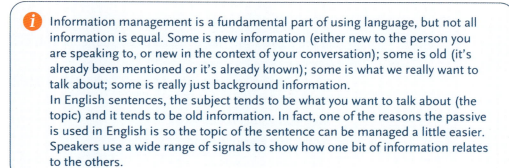 Information management is a fundamental part of using language, but not all information is equal. Some is new information (either new to the person you are speaking to, or new in the context of your conversation); some is old (it's already been mentioned or it's already known); some is what we really want to talk about; some is really just background information.

In English sentences, the subject tends to be what you want to talk about (the topic) and it tends to be old information. In fact, one of the reasons the passive is used in English is so the topic of the sentence can be managed a little easier. Speakers use a wide range of signals to show how one bit of information relates to the others.

2 3.3–3.7 **Listen to five brief excerpts. Which of the signals from Exercise 1 did you hear? Be careful: Excerpt 5 contains two signals.**

3 3.8–3.14 **Listen to these seven excerpts and identify which signal each speaker uses. Be careful: you won't find all of these signals in Exercise 1.**

Example: *I especially*

4 🎧 **3.8–3.14** Listen again, then work in pairs to place each of the signals in the correct category in Exercise 1.

Example: I especially (category 5)

5 🎧 **3.15** Listen to Margaret Lee, a marketing expert, giving a talk about brands and complete these extracts with the signals she uses.

1 Brands are _____ the way that companies have of identifying their products in the marketplace.

2 … and it focused on the connections between brands and globalization. _____ , I should say that it focused on the negative influence of big brands …

3 Anti-brand books, _____ the classic *The Hidden Persuaders*, have been around since the 1950s.

4 … in an advertisement of any sensory stimuli not designed to be perceived consciously. _____ , subliminal advertising is adding words or images that are targeted at your subconscious …

5 Historically, the concept of a brand as we mean it – which, _____ , is the concept of an identification for your particular product in the mass market …

6 … distribution networks greatly expanded, as a result of steam ships and railroads, and, _____ , the spread of industrialization broke the one-on-one relationships …

6 Add the signals you heard in Exercise 5 to the table in Exercise 1.

7 🎧 **3.15** Margaret uses other signals in her talk. Listen again and identify the signals she uses to …

1 show something is important

2 return to a previous topic

3 move on to a new topic

4 show that what follows is the answer to a question.

> ℹ️ Remember that signals are a dynamic part of language. That means that there are a number of variations, and the signals can change fairly rapidly. Don't be surprised if you hear something slightly different.

Listening for production

Working with summaries

 Summaries are a good way to improve your listening comprehension and practise your note-taking skills. Summaries require you to identify key ideas and recognize details, which is why teachers (and examiners) like to use them with high-level students.

A good summary:
1 clearly identifies the topic
2 clearly identifies key ideas
3 contains a few important or interesting details
4 reports what you heard, not what you think about it
5 is not a dictation; you should use your own words as much as possible
6 is brief.

A common listening activity asks you to complete a summary of what you have heard.

Before you listen, you should:
● look at the gaps so you know what kind of information to listen for
● note which key ideas the summary uses for organization, so you have a good idea of context. Remember that the information in the summary may not be in the order you heard it.

While you listen, you should:
● take notes rather than try to answer the questions directly.

After you listen, you should:
● look carefully at the structure of the sentences before you fill in the gaps. Quite often the sentence structure in the summary will be different from what you heard. You might need to change the word form (from verb to noun, for example) or make a passive verb active, etc.

1 🎧 3.15 **Listen again to Margaret Lee's talk and work in pairs to identify the topic and key ideas.**

2 **Look at this summary of Margaret's talk. Can you find your topic and key ideas? How is the summary organized? (Ignore the gaps for now.)**

> Brands have one very important function: they allow companies **1** _____ their products. The concept of brands dates back to the **2** _____ , when the spread of **3** _____ broke the direct relationships with producers and merchants that consumers had enjoyed.
>
> These days, the concept of brands does not enjoy a positive image. *No Logo*, which was published in **4** _____ , highlighted the relationship between big brands and **5** _____ , and focused on the negative influence big brands have.
>
> But *No Logo* was not the first anti-brand book. Published in the 1950s, **6** _____ introduced many people to the concept of subliminal advertising. In subliminal advertising, advertisers include in the advertisement sensory stimuli, generally **7** _____ or **8** _____ , that are not supposed to be perceived by your consciousness.

3 🎧 3.15 **Listen again and complete the summary.**

Listening for meaning

Unfamiliar vocabulary

 When listening to native speakers, it is unlikely that you will know every word and phrase they use. As long as you have a good command of the most common English words and phrases, you will probably understand the general meaning of what they are saying. But if you want to understand all the details, you will need to use some strategies for working with unfamiliar vocabulary. One important strategy is noticing how the words are formed. Does the speaker use prefixes that give you some idea of what the words mean? For instance, look at this excerpt from Track 3.15: ... *subliminal advertising is adding words or images that are targeted at your subconscious, and not your conscious.* You may not be familiar with the word *subconscious*, but if you are familiar with the prefix *sub–* and know that it means 'below', you can generate a good idea of what your subconscious is.

Another important strategy is paying attention to the other words and phrases that are being used with the unfamiliar item. In Track 3.2, for example, you hear *The website offered merchandise, including T-shirts, thongs, mouse pads and cookies.* You may not be familiar with the word *merchandise*, but the fact that the merchandise includes things like T-shirts, thongs, etc., and that these things were being offered by a website, can give you the idea that merchandise is stuff that is for sale.

You can sometimes use these two strategies together. You may notice, for example, that *merchandise* is similar to the more familiar word *merchant*. And you may notice that *subliminal* and *subconscious* share the *sub–* prefix and seem to refer to similar things.

Remember, you don't have to define the word or phrase precisely. You simply have to have some idea of what it means.

1 **The words in *italics* feature in audio tracks from this unit. Choose the most appropriate answer (a, b, c or d) for each question. (If necessary, use the audio transcripts on pages 101–102 to see the full context.)**

Track 3.2

1 'Well, according to the website, the aim was to increase the empathy people feel for – and I quote – the much-maligned rat.'

If people are *maligning* you, they are …

a trying to replace you.

b outlawing you.

c saying bad things about you.

d organizing an advertising campaign against you.

2 'In fact, they ran a print ad that had a drawing of a little girl cuddling a puppy.'

Which of the following is the best example of *cuddling*?

a a husband and wife holding each other in front of a fire

b a young boy playing catch with a ball

c a cat chasing its tail

d a bear putting its arms around a tree

3 '… and quite a few people in the advertising world are convinced that it was a hoax designed to highlight some ad agency.'

In this context, a *hoax* is most likely to be …

a a type of advertisement that relies on animals.

b a way to target people subliminally.

c something that is designed to deceive people.

d an illegal marketing method.

4 '… that the older sales pitch of preventing any more World War IIs just didn't resonate any more.'

What does the phrase *sales pitch* mean?

a the presentation sales people use to get you to buy something

b the proof that you get that you have purchased something

c the competitive advantage enjoyed by goods or a service

d the informal term used to describe the terms of a treaty or contract

Track 3.3

5 '… but in the US, universities have quite a bit of latitude in deciding what their requirements for a degree are …'

What is the best substitute for the word *latitude*?

a longitude

b success

c interest

d flexibility

Track 3.9

6 'The word "motto" comes from Italian, and it was originally a pledge.'

If you make a *pledge* to give money to a charity, you …

a request assistance because you don't have money.

b make a promise to give money.

c offer to consider donating some money.

d allow somebody to borrow your money.

Track 3.15

7 'But *No Logo* wasn't the first book to take brands to task.'

What do you do if you *take someone to task*?

a write a book about them

b work for them

c criticize them

d feel sorry for them

8 '… people went through advertisements with a fine-tooth comb, trying to spot the subliminal messages.'

What do you do if you *go through something with a fine-tooth comb*?

a look at something very carefully

b check that there is nothing illegal

c make sure that everything is neat

d split hairs about the meaning of something

2 **Here are four more excerpts from the audio transcripts. Work in pairs to explain what the expressions in *italics* mean.**

1 'But no one ever admitted to it, and they *went to great lengths* to make it seem legitimate …' (Track 3.2)

2 'There are so many different ways to rebrand […] that it's really hard to give *a blanket answer*.' (Track 3.2)

3 'Well, pizza and I *go way back together*.' (Track 3.11)

4 'The word "brand" has become a bit of *a dirty word* in recent years …' (Track 3.15)

> **⊸O Going further**
> Which of the words and phrases from Exercises 1 and 2 would you like to add to your productive vocabulary? Choose three of them and write your own sentence for each one. Then make sure you use each of them in a sentence (either written or spoken) every day for a week. See, too, if you can find them being used on the Internet. After one week, do you feel more confident when you use them?

Unit extension

1 **3.16 Listen to the continuation of Margaret Lee's talk and answer these questions.**

1 What point does Margaret make about shop owners in the big cities of the USA and the UK?

2 What does she use Shaker's soup as an example of?

3 How many advertisements is it estimated that people see each day?

4 What term does Margaret prefer to *advertisements*?

5 What point is she making when she compares Shaker's soup to Bohnen, My Tie and the other canned-soup brands on the market?

6 What did researchers start to look at after World War II?

7 Why does Margaret mention Bowl-a-Soup?

8 According to her, why are brands still important?

2 a What three or four ideas do you think are key ideas in the talk in Exercise 1? Write them out in complete sentences.

b Compare your choices with a partner's. Do you still agree with your choices?

3 Look at these two possible organizations for a summary of the talk. Which one is closer to your ideas from Exercise 2? Which one better represents the talk?

A

- Brands' big advantages
- Brands' big disadvantages
- Brands and globalization
- Margaret Lee's optimism

B

- Why brands developed
- Problems faced by brands
- A new direction for brands
- Margaret Lee's optimism

4 A good summary includes both key ideas and a small number of important and/or interesting details. Look back at your answers to the questions in Exercise 1 and your sentences from Exercise 2. Can you find one or two details to illustrate each key idea?

5 Work with a partner to write a brief summary of Margaret Lee's talk in Tracks 3.15 and 3.16.

> **i** Remember that summaries are brief. A good rule of thumb is to keep your summary to no more than one-third the length of the original source. Together, Tracks 3.15 and 3.16 are 992 words long, so try to keep your summary to around 300 words.

Consolidation 2

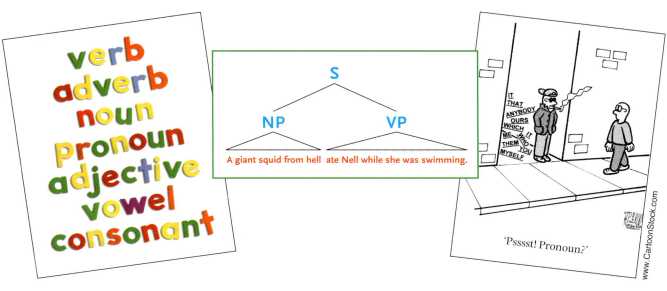

Topic focus

1 Work in pairs to place these linguistic terms in the diagram below.

base word	consonant	gender
object	preposition	pronoun
stress	subject	suffix
syllable	tense	verb

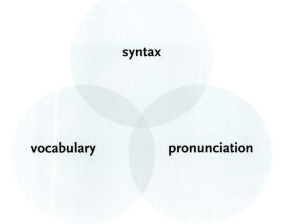

2 Do you think such terms are helpful when you are learning a language? Are there other linguistic features that you would like to learn the term for?

3 In pairs, discuss whether you agree or disagree with this statement, and why.

People who grow up speaking English think differently from people who grow up speaking my language.

Vocabulary focus

1 Match each of these words or phrases from this unit (1–12) with its definition (a–l).

1 universal		**a** to have as a result	
2 to attribute		**b** to give new life to	
3 one-off		**c** shared feature	
4 to turn out		**d** not living	
5 meticulous		**e** something that happens once	
6 reference		**f** to create a positive emotion	
7 to point out		**g** something that points to something else	
8 caveat		**h** covering everything	
9 to revitalize		**i** to indicate	
10 commonality		**j** to see something as a characteristic or cause of	
11 inanimate		**k** very thorough	
12 to strike a chord		**l** warning	

2 Use eight of the words and phrases from Exercise 1 to complete these sentences. You may need to change the form slightly.

1 Allow me to _____ that many of these vocabulary items are not all that commonly used.

2 Let me leave you with this _____ : never believe an email that asks for your personal data. It may very well be a phishing attempt.

3 We _____ our success to the fact that we hire only the very best.

4 Uncle Jarvis went through every old comic book very _____ before he let us take them.

5 We don't see our award-winning performance as a _____ . We think we can reach that level on a regular basis.

6 Martina made _____ to maritime law in her talk on international fishing agreements, but I'm not really sure what she meant.

7 Jenna's description of what it was like to spend 26 days alone on a lifeboat without any social media really _____ with the audience.

8 They say that the speed of light is the _____ speed limit because it applies everywhere.

> ## Going further
> Write sentences for the remaining words/phrases (but don't include the words themselves). Exchange sentences with your partner. Can you each successfully complete each other's sentences?

Practise your listening

1 🎧 **3.17** Listen to a conversation between a student (Naomi) and a professor (Professor Aoun), and decide which three of these five ideas are key ideas in the conversation.

a Universal grammar looks at what elements all languages share.

b Japanese sentence structure is different from English sentence structure.

c Absolute universals are shared by every language.

d Pronouns are universal.

e Implicational universals and how they work

2 🎧 **3.17** Listen again and answer these questions.

1 What are two of the surface elements mentioned by Professor Aoun?

2 What are two of the syntactical universals identified by Professor Aoun?

3 What are two of the pronunciation universals identified by Professor Aoun?

4 What are affixes?

5 Explain the concept of implicational universals.

6 What is Professor Aoun's argument in favour of language universals?

3 This is the beginning and the end of a summary of the conversation between Professor Aoun and Naomi. Use your answers from Exercises 1 and 2 to write two paragraphs to complete it.

> Despite the fact that different languages have different grammars, there is evidence to suggest that languages also share some commonalities. The term used to refer to those elements shared by all languages is 'language universals'.

> Some experts remain unconvinced that language universals exist, pointing to the fact that there remain languages that have not been fully studied. Nevertheless, the fact that humans throughout the world have similar brains, and learn their first language in the same way, suggests that language universals could very well exist.

🔍 Going further

How many linguistic terms do you know? Match these clues with terms you heard in Track 3.17.

1 the study of language *linguistics*
2 not feminine
3 the units of a spoken word
4 passive subject in an active sentence
5 *b, c, w, r, s, p,* etc.
6 something added to the end of a word
7 e.g. *for, to, on, beyond*
8 something regularly repeated
9 e.g. E-I-E-I-O
10 distinctive characteristic or attribute

1 **Look at this transcript of a radio commentary on dying languages. There are ten signals missing. Discuss in pairs what you think they are.**

> How should we respond to the death of a language? We open our newspapers one morning and find out that one more last speaker has died, carrying with them the last remnants of Bo or Eyak. The article will mention one or two vocabulary items that the world will never hear again, **1** _____ *demex'ch*, which means 'a soft spot in the ice that is good for fishing', and then point out that many of the world's 6,000 plus languages are in danger of fading away. **2** _____ , one news report claimed that up to 90% of the world's languages will be extinct by the end of this century.
>
> **3** _____ these linguistic deaths are reported in sombre tones, **4** _____ we cannot stop some languages from going extinct, and, **5** _____ we could, I'm not sure we should. Languages, **6** _____ , have been dying for as long as we have been speaking. The history of language is the history of language death.
>
> Critics will respond that we are losing linguistic diversity at an increasing rate. A recent Language Census counted 6,906 living languages. It **7** _____ noted that 91 other languages had 'gone out of use' since the previous census, just four years earlier. Another 1,038 languages have fewer than a thousand speakers.
>
> **8** _____ , there are 389 languages that have at least one million speakers. **9** _____ it turns out that those languages are spoken by 94% of the people on Earth. **10** _____ , even if 90% of today's languages did disappear, there would still be more than 600 languages around for us to speak. An in every one of them there will be some way of talking about a soft spot in the ice that is good for fishing.

2 🎧 **3.18 Listen and write down the 12 signals you hear. How many of the signals you chose in Exercise 1 are on the list?**

3 **Complete the transcript in Exercise 1 using ten of the signals you heard in Exercise 2.**

4 🎧 **3.19 Listen to a talk about dying languages and complete each gap in this transcript with up to three words from the recording.**

Why do languages die?

The simplistic answer is that a language dies because it **1** _____ native speakers. The reason this answer is simplistic is because it does not offer an explanation **2** _____ people have stopped speaking the language.

3 _____ language death is usually a gradual one. A community becomes bilingual and, **4** _____ from its original language to the new one. Eventually, the people of the community stop using their native tongue altogether. This assimilation, **5** _____ called, can bring about the death of the native language.

Why does the **6** _____ the new language? Economic and social reasons are **7** _____ list. People, particularly adults, communicate to a large degree in order to **8** _____ and to socialize. Once a new language becomes the language of business and social contact, the older language can quickly find itself in danger.

Is **9** _____ language a dying language? Not necessarily. There have been efforts to revitalize a number of languages, including Hebrew, Welsh and even Navajo. How successful these efforts have been is **10** _____ , but it's clear that a dying language strikes a chord and makes us reflect on what language means to us.

5 These notes refer to a talk about linguistic determinism. Work in pairs to determine what the abbreviations might mean or refer to.

Linguistic determinism

1 Basics
Def.: Lang. tells us what we can/c'not **1** ....
Scient. basis devlp'd in **2** ....
AKA: **3** ....
LD: lang. structure limits what we can understand
   – Claim: spkrs of Hopi **4** .... the way it is understood in Eng.

2 Problems w/ S-W
W's research
   – only interviewed **5** .... (in NYC!)
S-W too strong

3 6 ....
Lang. = info. mgmt (mostly)
   – lots of info. in reality
   – Language select info.
      – must pay attn to some/can't pay attn to all
      – ex: Eng. don't pay attn to how well you **7** .... (Fr. yes)

4 Experiment
   – Fr. v. Germ. v. Span. (contrasting genders: masc./fem.)
   8 .... (Germ. = fem. = elegance/Sp. = masc. = strength)

---

6 🎧 **3.20** Listen and complete the gaps in the notes above with up to four words in each gap. Do the abbreviations match what you thought they meant?

> ⓘ Remember that notes are not permanent records. The best way to make sure that your notes are used well is to review them soon after you take them. Then write out – in complete sentences – the information you think is important, and take note of any information you don't understand well.
> Taking a few minutes at the end of the day will save you a lot of time later, because you won't have to figure out what you meant or why you made the note in the first place.

7 🎧 **3.20** Listen again and add information you think is important to this mind map.

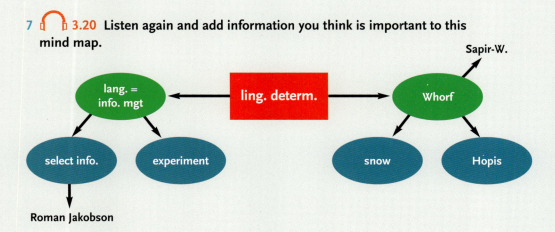

8 Here are 12 words from Track 3.20. Ten of them can be found on the Academic Word List. Discuss in pairs which two you think are *not* part of the AWL.

alternative	available	concept	finite
flow	gender	hypothesis	linguistics
precisely	published	requires	sex

Pairwork material

Unit 1, Language focus, Exercise 4

Student A

1 The company I work for has 359,764 employees worldwide.

2 The Museum of Contemporary Art just paid 99,812,000 dollars for a painting by Picasso.

3 Last month, the pizzeria my cousin owns sold 3,052 mushroom pizzas.

4 My company lost 7.83 billion dollars last year.

5 I was going to buy Ivan's old car, but he wanted 4,500 euros for it.

6 A light year is equal to 9,460,730,472,580.8 kilometres.

Unit 2, Listening for production, Exercise 3

Student A

a Read this report from the band's manager to Student B.

Well, we've had a chance to look at the numbers from the Canadian leg of your North American Reunion Tour, and I thought you'd want to know how things stand. As I'm sure you'll remember, we began the tour in British Columbia and spent four weeks in western Canada before moving east towards Ontario. Short Shrift played a total of 12 shows in Vancouver, Calgary and Banff. We hadn't originally planned to spend all that time in western Canada; in fact, we had planned on starting the tour in Washington and Oregon, but as you know, there were some problems, and we weren't able to get American visas in time.

For ten shows in the middle of the tour, Short Shrift was the opening band for the Funky Knights. I know you were happy to spend a few days helping them out with their comeback tour, but I have to be honest and say that being the opening act for the Funky Knights was not a very profitable decision. In the end, the Canadian tour grossed somewhere around 1.2 million Canadian dollars, but you could have grossed more if you had been the headliners for the whole tour.

b Listen to Student B and answer the even-numbered questions from Exercise 2.

Student A
1 Read the extract below carefully.
2 Write three sentence-completion questions about it for Student B. Be clear if you want to limit the number of words Student B can use to complete each sentence.
3 Give Student B the questions and read your extract aloud twice.
4 Correct Student B's answers.

One school of thought is what we call the 'constitutive' school of thought. The constitutive school of thought says that sovereign states are those states that other sovereign states recognize as sovereign states. If the other sovereign states don't say you're sovereign, well, then, you're not sovereign.

This is a rather old-fashioned school of thought. It comes out of 19th-century Europe, a development of all the political games that took place after the fall of Napoleon, and its effect was to protect the interest of the great European powers. Indeed, you can picture a group of 19th-century European diplomats sipping brandies over a map and saying, 'Well, yes, we can recognize this sovereign state, but of course we can't recognize that other one because it wouldn't be in the interest of our friend over there in the corner.' It's not all that different from what happens in many high-school cafeterias today.

Student A
Listen to the talk again, then complete these notes using no more than three words or a number in each gap.

Eaton study looked at **1** .... occupations
One possible reason x depression rate: lawyers trained **2** .... risk
Martin Seligman says reason x success at Law Schl might be that
    pessimists = more **3** ....
Pessimism at work: anticipating **4** ....
Even **5** .... have more standing than lawyers
Pessimism not always inappropriate – pessimists see reality **6** ....

Student B

1 I work for a big company, too. Overall, we have 287,174 employees.

2 I made 2,700 euros when I sold the painting that my grandfather left me.

3 My sister-in-law is so mathematical that she always cuts her steak-and-kidney pie into 3.14 slices.

4 A woman I know who works on Wall Street made 22,518,000 dollars last year.

5 With tax, the price of my motorcycle was 5,412 euros.

6 If you use imperial measurements, a light year is equal to 5,878,625,373,183.6 miles.

Student B
a Listen to Student A and answer the odd-numbered questions from Exercise 2.
b Read this report from the band's manager to Student A.

Well, we've had a chance to look at the numbers from the Canadian leg of your North American Reunion Tour, and I thought you'd want to know how things stand. As I'm sure you'll remember, we began the tour in February and spent about a month in western Canada before we started moving east towards Ontario. Altogether, Short Shrift played a total of 29 shows in Canada, and seeing as how you hadn't done a tour in over four years, I have to say I think you played pretty well.

On the other hand, you still have a bit of work to do if you want to get back to the good old days of the 'Get Shorty' tour. You only sold out one show – the one in Montreal – and I have a feeling that the people in Montreal came out because they heard that Corky Laing would be playing with you.

In the end, the tour was a little bit in the red. We wound up losing roughly 150,000 Canadian dollars, but I won't have the exact numbers for another week. Don't worry, though, because we have a plan to generate more revenue from the tour. We're going to sell the music from the shows online, at around six dollars per download. And that should help the tour turn a profit.

Student B
1 Read the extract below carefully.
2 Write three sentence-completion questions about it for Student A. Be clear if you want to limit the number of words Student A can use to complete each sentence.
3 Give Student A the questions and read your extract aloud twice.
4 Correct Student A's answers.

The declarative school of thought is a bit more modern. This might sound more democratic. The state stands up and declares that it is free, and *voilà*, we have a new sovereign state. Unfortunately, the declaration in the declarative school of thought does not come from our would-be state. No, what the declarative school of thought says is that we have a sovereign state any time a set of criteria is met, regardless of whether or not the other sovereign states have recognized the state. In the declarative school, recognition is merely 'declarative', it does not change your status.

But there is a problem: there is more than one set of criteria. Different people, different bodies use different criteria. One set often used is the criteria of the Montevideo Convention. Now, it's true that the Montevideo Convention was agreed in 1933, which was a long time ago, or so it seems; on the other hand, Article 1 of the Convention lists a total of four criteria, which is quite modern in its simplicity, a sort of Apple computer of international law.

Student B
Listen to the talk again, then complete these notes using no more than three words or a number in each gap.

> Lawyers **1** _____ times more depressed than gnrl popul. according to Eaton study
> One possible reason x depression rate: lawyers trained to figure out ways to **2** _____
> Univ. **3** _____ study: pessimists outperform optimists (opp. of nrml)
> Martin Seligman = important figure in field of **4** _____
> Low standing in community > **5** _____
> Pessimists = better **6** _____ evaluators

Academic Word List exercises

Unit 1

The speaker from Track 1.13 went on to talk about other university courses that can make you rich. Complete the extract below using the words from the box.

> aspect   assumptions   commit   communicate
> conclusion   consequences   errors   finally
> requires   tasks   valuable   wise

So the question the young lady asked was, 'Which other courses do you recommend?'

Certainly, I think you need to take a history course. History can be boring. But if you look at history from a different viewpoint, it can open doors for you. The most valuable **1** _____ of history is its ability to show us where other people went wrong. Studying history helps you learn from their mistakes so that, hopefully, you won't **2** _____ the same mistakes.

Think of all the terrible decisions you can find in history. All of the unintended **3** _____ . All of the mistaken **4** _____ . Look at these **5** _____ and figure out how a better decision could have been made. Then, apply that realization to today's world and to your own situation.

And think of all the people who rose to the occasion. The inspirational leaders, the **6** _____ decision-makers. How did they inspire? How did they manage to come to the right **7** _____ ? What can you learn from them?

Take a course on management, too. It's amazing how many bosses really have no idea how to manage their people. Running anything **8** _____ you to **9** _____ effectively and efficiently. You need to explain **10** _____ and decisions to employees. Not only will the people under you have a clearer understanding of why they are doing what they are doing, they'll probably like you more as well.

11 _____ , in spite of the stereotype of English majors and long careers in the fast-food industry, take a literature course. Literature, like

history, is full of **12** _____ lessons. What can you learn from Shakespeare's King Lear about leadership, or Hemingway's Frederic Henry about resilience?

Literature gives you the chance to learn the lessons we've talked about in these other courses. Studying good writers can make you a better writer, for example, as long as you take the time to pay attention. Tom Wolfe's *The Bonfire of the Vanities* can teach you a lot about how Wall Street works.

⚲ Going further
Ten of the 12 words you used are on the Academic Word List. Can you identify which two are not? Do you think they are words you need to know?

Read this passage about the economics of Woodstock. Each of the 12 gaps contains part of a word. Sometimes it is the first part, sometimes it is the second part. Complete the words.

It is easy to lose sight of the fact that Woodstock was **1** desi_____ to be a money-making enterprise. The **2** prom_____ had sold $1.3 million worth of tickets before the event, and only took the decision to turn it into a free concert when it became clear that there would be serious **3** _____rity concerns if they did not **4** rem_____ the fences around the concert site.

The festival itself was quite unprofitable. At the end of the weekend, John Roberts, one of the four organizers, had written $600,000 worth of cheques he could not cover, and total expenses had amounted to $2.6 million, far in excess of the $500,000 which had originally been **5** proj_____ .

Starting the day after the concert, the situation improved, **6** _____eit slowly. Roberts's father lent him the money to pay for the uncovered cheques. In September, two of Woodstock Ventures's **7** _____nders – Michael Lang and Artie Kornfeld – were bought out.

1970 saw the **8** rele_____ of the documentary film *Woodstock*. Produced on a budget of just $600,000, over the years the film has grossed more than $50 million.

9 Non_____ , Woodstock did not break even for almost a **10** _____ade. Part of the reason is that Woodstock Ventures received $1 million and only a small **11** _____tage of the profits for the **12** distr_____ rights to the film.

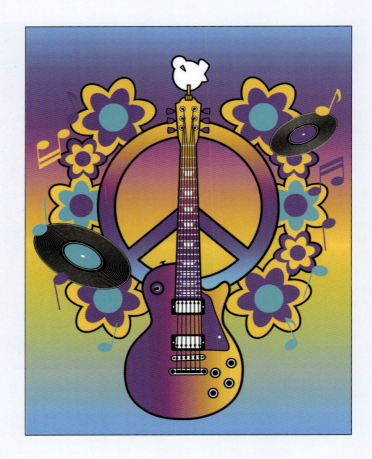

Read this passage about Sealand's sovereignty and choose the best answer below (a, b, c or d) for each gap.

Is Sealand truly a sovereign state? According to the Montevideo Convention, a sovereign state must possess four qualifications: a permanent population, **1** _____ territory, a government and the **2** _____ to enter into relations with other states.

Since 1987, the British government has included Sealand within its territorial waters. **3** _____, a 1968 decision by a British court that Sealand lay outside British territorial waters could be **4** _____ as **5** _____ of sovereignty.

But that is not enough to satisfy the Montevideo conditions. It is easy enough for Sealand to satisfy the second condition, as the extent of its territory is well established. The third condition – the existence of a government – is also **6** _____. Indeed, Sealand boasts a written **7** _____.

It is the fourth condition – **8** _____ with other states – that is open to **9** _____. In its defence, Sealand **10** _____ the fact that it has often had dealings with the British government. It also points to its curious dealings with the West German government in 1978. After a failed coup d'état in Sealand, a German citizen was charged with treason. After the British government refused requests to get **11** _____, a West German diplomat travelled from London to negotiate the prisoner's **12** _____. Sealand claims that this negotiation was, in fact, recognition of Sealand's sovereignty.

	a	b	c	d
1	an assumed	an internal	a reliable	a defined
2	capacity	factor	evidence	role
3	Whereas	Nevertheless	Furthermore	Thereby
4	interpreted	assured	administrated	impacted
5	linkage	evidence	output	relevance
6	overall	liberating	straightforward	imprecise
7	constitution	license	ministry	utility
8	equipment	hierarchies	interactions	occupation
9	diminution	detection	debate	disposal
10	transmits	cites	advocates	rationalises
11	consulted	assigned	enforced	involved
12	externalization	release	sustenance	inhibition

Read this passage about another threat to the Earth and do the exercises that follow.

Back in 2004, an asteroid was discovered **1** _____ 40 million kilometres from Earth. As scientists began to calculate the asteroid's orbit, they were **?** alarmed to discover that on April 13th, 2029, the asteroid will pass so close to Earth that it will actually be closer than our **2** _____ satellites.

? how close it will come, scientists are now confident that the asteroid – named Apophis – will not hit the Earth in 2029. This confidence is based on the **3** _____ of the calculations of Apophis's orbit. What could have been a disaster will instead be an opportunity, for Apophis will be the largest near-Earth object ever observed.

But the story of Apophis does not end here. Apophis's orbit will bring it back to the Earth's neighbourhood seven years later. And **?** scientists are confident that Apophis will miss the Earth in 2029, they are not as certain about 2036.

When Apophis passes by in 2029, there is a **4** _____ of trajectories it can take, and within that **5** _____ , there is a 600-metre **6** _____ , the **7** _____ 'keyhole'. Should Apophis pass through the keyhole, then when it returns in 2036, it will collide with the Earth.

It has even determined where Apophis would hit the Earth: the Pacific Ocean, west of California.

Aphophis is far smaller than the asteroid that caused the extinction of the dinosaurs. **?**, its **8** _____ would be **9** _____ . It would cause tsunami that could devastate California's coast.

Fortunately, the **10** _____ that Apophis will return to hit the Earth are small. And even if it turns out that Apophis does pass through the keyhole, there are steps that we can take to **11** _____ the threat.

It is important to remember that it is not necessary to destroy Apophis. As long as it is not on a collision course with Earth, it really does not matter where Apophis is in space. So, **12** _____ , a rocket sent to intercept Apophis and crash into it would deflect the asteroid enough from its trajectory to miss the Earth.

1 **There are four question marks (?) in the passage. Which four of these five function words from the Academic Word List can replace the question marks?**

despite   likewise   nevertheless   somewhat   whereas

2 **Complete ten of the gaps in the passage using ten of the 12 words in the box below. Then complete the other two gaps with a word from the Academic Word List on your own. (Hint: The same word will complete both gaps.)**

approximately	area	communications	impact
odds	option	precision	remove
significant	so-called	scope	theoretically

Complete each gap in this passage with the appropriate form of the word in brackets. (The words in brackets all come from the Academic Word List.)

The human brain has changed quite a bit in the past two million years. One of the key **1** _____ (*innovate*) in the make-up of the brain has been the development of the pre-frontal cortex. The pre-frontal cortex allows us to **2** _____ (*simulation*) experience, to imagine a future that has not yet arrived.

In an experiment, psychologist Dan Gilbert asked **3** _____ (*voluntary*) whether they would prefer to win the lottery or lose the use of their legs. It is the pre-frontal cortex that allowed them to weigh the two outcomes and determine which would make them happier.

The 'correct' choice seems obvious, but it turns out that there is very little difference: after one year, both lottery winners and paraplegics were equally happy, according to Gilbert.

This is because the pre-frontal cortex is not a particularly **4** _____ (*accuracy*) simulator. Events do not **5** _____ (*affective*) us the way we think they will. They will not last as long as we think they will. They will not be as **6** _____ (*intensity*) as we think they will.

This position is not **7** _____ (*controversy*). Many people **8** _____ (*rejection*) the idea that negative outcomes do not make us unhappy. The key, according to Gilbert, is what he calls 'synthetic happiness'. This is the ability to change our world view so that we are happier with the world we **9** _____ (*residence*) in. Synthetic happiness, in other words, is the happiness we make when we would otherwise be unhappy. **10** _____ (*dramatic*) the impact of a future outcome is known as the 'impact bias'. In a certain sense, it is a negative **11** _____ (*adapt*) in the human brain. Synthetic happiness, on the other hand, is a sign of how **12** _____ (*resources*) our brains can be in generating a positive world for us to live in.

Read this excerpt from a presentation on rebranding the Democratic Republic of Bognor and answer the questions below.

Good morning. And thank you for allowing us to take part in your 'Rebrand Bognor' workshop. I'd like to start by exploring this concept of rebranding a nation.

A nation, after all, isn't a can of soda pop or a laundry detergent. So how can we say that it's a brand? But then, nations have an **A** _____ , just like products. A few years ago, there was a joke about heaven and hell in Europe, where all the lovers in heaven were Italian, the cooks were French and everything was organized by the Swiss, while in hell, all the mechanics were French, the cooks were English and everything was organized by the Italians. In other words, France projects an **A** _____ of good food and bad mechanics.

So, nation rebranding is about evaluating the **A** _____ that your country projects, and making changes when they are necessary. Now, let me say a few words about these changes. You, of course, can choose the **A** _____ for Bognor that you want, but it's important to be realistic. If you make unrealistic claims, your rebranding efforts will not be successful.

So where does your brand **A** _____ come from? From a number of sources. First, the **A** _____ is generated by **B** _____ with the people of the country. When I say that, everyone assumes I mean tourism, and of course tourism is an important means of exposure, but tourism is not the only way we **C** _____ with people from other nations. In fact, most of our **B** _____ come about because of people we meet in our homes, or meet in a public way,

through politicians, say, or even through media such as movies or music. It is those **B** _____ that make us willing to be tourists to that country in the first place. People want to travel to Italy after they have eaten a fine meal at an Italian restaurant at home, not before.

Another major source of a country's **A** _____ is its government. Or better, its governmental institutions. What's it like to deal with the bureaucracy, for example? Is it easy for business people to do business there, or do they get tied up in red **D** _____ ? What's the diplomacy like?

1 Look at this sentence from paragraph 1: *And thank you for allowing us to take part in your 'Rebrand Bognor' workshop.* Which word from the Academic Word List can be used instead of *take part*?

2 There are seven gaps labelled 'A' in this passage. Which word from the Academic Word List goes in all seven gaps?

3 In paragraph 4, there are three gaps labelled 'B'. Which word from the Academic Word List goes in all three gaps?

4 In paragraph 4, there is a gap labelled 'C'. Which word from the Academic Word List goes in the gap? (Hint: it is a form of the word in gap B.)

5 In paragraph 5, there is a gap labelled 'D'. Which word from the Academic Word List completes the expression

Audio transcripts

UNIT 1

Track 1.1

1 If you go to see Dr Allen during her office hours, she'll be glad to go over your writing assignment with you and show you where you made your mistakes.

Track 1.2

2 The tuition at this college is quite expensive, but more than three-quarters of students receive some form of financial aid, so please don't assume that you'll have to pay the full amount.

Track 1.3

3 Are you sure you can take Advanced Economic Theory without taking Macro- and Micro-Economics first? I thought they were prerequisites.

Track 1.4

4 I won't be on campus next fall, because I'll be at a law firm in Chicago, doing an internship – my professor says it'll help my chances of getting into law school.

Track 1.5

5 We're very proud to announce that Cynthia Lee is the winner of this year's $5,000 Dorfman Scholarship for Academic Excellence, which I hear she'll be using to attend Faber College. Congratulations, Cynthia.

Track 1.6

6 But Professor Callahan, you can't give me a D Minus for American History! A grade that low will ruin my grade point average!

Track 1.7

7 This semester, we'll be focusing on geologic periods, such as the Jurassic and the Triassic. Then, next semester, we'll look at how geology affects today's world.

Track 1.8

8 You'll be taking two major exams this term. The final will be the week before Christmas and will count for 30% of your final grade. There'll also be a mid-term, which will be sometime around Halloween, and that'll count for 20% of your grade.

Track 1.9

Alan: Hello everybody, and welcome to this week's segment of *Your Educational Life*. According to statistics, 15.9 million students will head off to American universities this year, working towards their degrees. Not all of those students are American, either. Currently, there are 582,984 foreign students registered in the US. Many of our listeners hope to join those students and earn an American university degree.
But what exactly does that mean? The system may make sense to Americans, but for those of us outside the United States, the difference between a college and a university, or between a Bachelor of Arts and a Bachelor of Science degree, can be just as confusing as the rules of baseball. To help us with our confusion, I've asked the Dean of Admissions of Faber College, Dawn Liebowitz,

to explain how the American system works. Dr Liebowitz, thanks so much for joining us today.

Dawn: It's my pleasure, Alan.

Alan: Faber College is in Oregon, isn't it?

Dawn: That's right.

Alan: How many of all those foreign students is Faber home to?

Dawn: Roughly 1,600, which doesn't sound like very much, I know. But Faber is not a big college. We only have about 8,000 students total, so foreign students actually make up 20% of our student body. Of course, a lot of them are from Canada, but Canada does count.

Alan: Twenty per cent is quite a large percentage, even if they are Canadians, isn't it?

Dawn: It is, but Faber has – since its founding in 1948 – followed what we call our open-door policy, and so we've always been quite active in recruiting foreign students to come to Faber.

Alan: And as the Dean of Admissions at Faber, I assume that you have a lot to do with all that recruiting. What exactly does a Dean of Admissions do?

Dawn: Well, as the name implies, my office is responsible for getting students into Faber. Of course, it's much more complicated than that. We start with the applications … well, actually, we start with the recruitment, and then we process the applications. Then there's the selection process, then we work with the students to determine what financial aid they can get, and, finally, there's the enrolment, when they all actually become Faber students.

Alan: Just in that brief description you've touched on a number of issues that I think our listeners find confusing. But before we get into those, let me ask you a question about the name of your school. Faber College, not Faber University. Why? What's the difference between a college and a university?

Dawn: Technically, not very much, because there isn't a precise distinction in the United States. Basically, *college* is the general term we use when we want to talk about the school that students go to after they graduate from high school. We'll ask, 'Where did you go to college?', say, or talk about 'saving money for college'. We don't really use the word *university* in contexts like that. More precisely, *college* usually refers to your undergraduate studies, not to a Master's degree or a doctorate, and colleges tend to be smaller than universities.

Alan: So, you mentioned undergraduate studies and degrees. Could you tell us a little about how degrees work in America?

Dawn: Generally, when you talk about 'college' in America, what people have in mind is a four-year school, and when you graduate at the end of the four years, you get a Bachelor's degree, either a Bachelor of Arts or a Bachelor of Science.

Alan: Generally, but not exclusively?

Dawn: No. Some students can get a Bachelor of

Engineering, for example, or a Bachelor of Design. That depends on the institution awarding the degree. And of course, while the term *undergraduate* generally applies to a four-year college, there are also two-year colleges, which are usually called *community colleges* these days.

Alan: And they also award Bachelor's degrees?

Dawn: No. They award Associate degrees. These tend to be more vocational, more job-training oriented and less academic, though of course many community-college students do go on to attend a four-year college and earn their Bachelor's.

Alan: Now, when you get your Bachelor's degree, do you actually study 'arts' or 'science', or do you study something more specific?

Dawn: 'Arts' and 'science' are vague terms, aren't they? Arts, here, refers to the liberal arts, by the way, not things like painting or photography. The liberal arts, traditionally, are the seven areas of study that develop a student's intellect and rational thought.

Alan: Does that mean that American university students have to study rhetoric, for example, or astronomy?

Dawn: Or grammar, logic, geometry, math and music, to round out the traditional list of liberal-arts subjects. No, though many of the liberal arts still play a role in a college education. However, to get back to your question, American college students do study something more specific than 'arts' or 'science' – we call that something specific the student's 'major'. So you might graduate with a Bachelor of Arts in economics, say. And if your major is Economics, you'll take courses like Statistics and Macro-economics and also some higher-level courses like Behavioural Economics. On the other hand, if your major is Biochemistry, you'll wind up with a Bachelor of Science, and obviously take biology courses, like Molecular Biology and chemistry courses like Organic Chemistry, but you'll also need to take a course in Scientific Writing, because you won't get published unless you know how to write for scientific journals.

Alan: So a major is your specialization, then?

Dawn: More or less. I think 'concentration' is a better word myself, simply because while you do most of your studying in your major, you don't spend all of your time studying in it. And this is where the liberal-arts part of the discussion comes into play. In a lot of countries, students focus almost exclusively on one field of study when they get to university, but American students usually need to complete some kind of core curriculum, which includes classes in a number of different fields. The idea here is that students will be exposed to these different fields and different ways of thinking, and perhaps even find a new interest for their studies. Lots of American students actually change their majors after taking a core course, and some colleges actually stop students from declaring the major until they've taken a certain number of core courses.

Alan: Dr Liebowitz, I need to stop you there for a moment, because we need to take a break for station identification. When we come back, can I ask you about some college numbers?

Dawn: Of course, Alan.

Alan: You're listening to *Your Educational Life*. This is Alan Furst, and we'll be back in two minutes.

a forty-two million, three hundred and five
b eight billion, five hundred million
c sixty-seven hundred
d fifty-three thousand, one hundred and sixty-six
e two hundred and twelve thousand, three hundred and one

Track 1.11

1 Did you know that the largest employer in the world had 2,055,001 employees last year?
2 In the late 1980s, somebody bought Van Gogh's *Irises* for $53.9 million, but he didn't have the money to pay for it.
3 We need to sell 6,212 pieces of sushi every two weeks in order to break even.
4 My company made a $3.04 billion profit two years ago.
5 It cost me 8,200 euros to repair my car after the accident.
6 An astronomical unit, which is 149,597,870.7 kilometres, is the distance between the Earth and the Sun.

Track 1.12

Alan: Welcome back to *Your Educational Life*. I'm Alan Furst, and today we're talking to Dr Dawn Liebowitz, Dean of Admissions at Faber College, about college in America. Thank you again for taking the time to speak with us, Dr Liebowitz.

Dawn: Oh, you're welcome, Alan.

Alan: Now, I understand that you'd like to share some numbers with us.

Dawn: That's right, Alan. You know, Americans just love to quantify things, and so I thought I'd see if I can paint a picture of American colleges using numbers.

Alan: All right, well, away we go. What's the first number?

Dawn: Well, the first number is 1636, which is the year that the Massachusetts Bay Colony founded Harvard. However, it wasn't called that until March 13, 1639, when it was named after John Harvard, who had left his library of 400 books to the school, not to mention some much-needed cash. The second important number is 1642, which is the year that Harvard awarded its first Bachelor of Arts degrees to nine students. So while American universities may not have the history of a University of Cambridge or a University of Bologna, the system has been around for more than 360 years.

Alan: Good point. What are our next numbers?

Dawn: Well, the next number is 1,524,092, which is the number of Bachelor's degrees awarded by American colleges – and universities – in the last academic year, which is a lot different from nine.

Alan: 1,524,092. Wow!

Dawn: Plus, you need to consider that another 728,114 people received Associate degrees, so the total number of undergraduate degrees awarded in the United States last year was 2,252,206.

Alan: And where did all those people go to school?

Dawn: Well, it depends a little on how you count, but according to the federal government, last year there were 2,675 four-year institutions and 1,877 community colleges, or two-year institutions, so college students in America did have some choice.

Alan: I'll say! 'Four-year institution' does mean college or university, doesn't it?

Dawn: That's right. Remember that those terms don't have precise meanings in the States, so the official statistics refer to 'four-year institutions'.

Alan: So what are all these people studying?

Dawn: Well, Business is far and away the number-one field, with 327,531 Bachelor's degrees awarded, but the second most popular field was Social Sciences and History – there were close to 164,000 degrees awarded in that field – and the third biggest category was Education, which saw just over 105,000 degrees awarded. Oh, and for those of you who care about such things, the field with the fewest number of degrees awarded was Precision Production, with only 23 degrees, fewer even than Library Science – only 82 people left school with Library Science degrees.

Alan: I've never heard of Precision Production. What's that?

Dawn: It's basically artisanal production. Making things like furniture by hand, or glassworks, precision watches – anything that requires a high level of skill to produce.

Alan: Do many schools offer degrees in Precision Production?

Dawn: I really don't know the specific number. But I do know that a couple of big schools like Brigham Young and Michigan State offer programmes, and I know that professional degrees – degrees that train you to do a specific job – are becoming more popular.

Alan: We only have about 30 seconds left, Dr Liebowitz. Can I ask you for one last number?

Dawn: Yes. That number is $13,424. That was the average tuition at an American college or university last year. So, remember to choose your college carefully. It's quite an investment of both time and money.

Alan: It certainly is. Dr Dawn Liebowitz, thank you so much for being our guest today. This is Alan Furst, and you've been listening to *Your Educational Life*. Until next week, remember everybody, Knowledge is Good.

Track 1.13

Isn't it common knowledge that college doesn't prepare you well for the real world? Haven't we all heard stories of taxi drivers with Master's degrees and English majors tending bars? Maybe, but the truth is that there are several courses you can take, courses that will give you critical information and instruction. And if you can figure out how to use that information and that instruction correctly, you'll find yourself on the path to riches. So let's start off and talk about five courses that can make you rich.

The first course is Accounting. Although this list is in no particular order, I think Accounting is, by far, the most important course to take if you want to succeed financially. Too many people don't understand a balance sheet. They don't understand that if you go out and buy a 47-inch plasma TV set on credit, you haven't just purchased a cool new asset, you've also created a big new liability. What's an asset, what's a liability, you ask? This is why you need an Accounting course. If you want to be successful, you need to understand exactly what you own, and exactly what you owe. Learning the difference between assets and liabilities, as well as concepts like inventory and cashflow, is especially crucial if you want to start your own business. The health of a business is reflected in its balance sheet. As those numbers go, so does the business.

Next is Marketing. If you want to make money from selling something, then you need to be able to figure out what that something is. Marketing is the process of finding the right product to sell. Now, in itself, marketing is *not* selling. It's the process of promoting certain products and services. Taking a Marketing course will help you figure out what consumers want and how to come up with a product that satisfies those desires. Too often, products fail because their creators didn't bother to learn whether a market for the product even existed. They produced it, but not enough people bought it. Marketing teaches you to find the market first, and then develop the product.

Number three is Economics. I regret not taking Economics when I was in college. Understanding the production, distribution and consumption of goods and services lets you take a big-picture approach to business and investing. If you understand how the economy got to be where it is today, it helps you identify where your money should be. You can pick out the right investments and turn away from the bad ones. You can identify which direction your business should go in, and figure out how to take advantage of certain trends.

This leads to Finance. It's tax season, and several people you know are probably receiving refund cheques in the mail from the Internal Revenue Service. If you're excited about receiving a refund cheque, you probably never took a finance course. Receiving a refund is a way for you to lose money. The government took money from you and held on to that money for a year and they didn't pay you any interest. Thus, your money lost value during that time. How much value? Well, what's the inflation rate? You lost whatever the inflation rate was over the past year.

A Finance course would help you understand that. Finance teaches you that because prices go up – the rate of inflation, right? – your money doesn't buy as much today as it did this time last year. That's how the time value of money works.

One of the keys to becoming rich is really understanding how money works when it's not in your hands. A finance course (preferably one geared toward entrepreneurship) will teach you what you need to know to reach this level of understanding. There might be some math involved, but it won't kill you. It'll just make you stronger.

Number five is Writing and Composition. Succeeding as an entrepreneur requires that you be able to express yourself, your ideas. Whether it involves pitching an idea to an investor, writing a press release or composing a business plan, entrepreneurs need to communicate. More often than not, this communication is done in writing. Basic composition and grammar skills can do wonders for your ability to express what you have to say clearly and effectively.

Just glance around at the number of blogs across the Internet and you'll see a lot of bad writing. It's an instant turnoff and blocks people from focusing on what you're trying to say. Good writing, on the other hand, draws in a reader, and it gives you a shot at selling someone on your content. In other words, it helps you get in the door.

So there you have five courses that can make you rich. Next, we'll focus on what to do when you finish college.

UNIT 2

Track 1.14

Live music is big business. Concerts, or shows, are promoted by promoters, who find places for the performers to play. These venues – which can be small music clubs or huge stadiums – are usually booked by the promoter, who has to cover the rent and other expenses before the performers get paid. With all the expenses that promoters have to cover, bands will sometimes get paid very little, even if the concert grosses a large amount. Sometimes the promoter only promotes one show; other times, they promote a series of shows in different cities. This is known as a 'tour'. When a band goes on tour, they will often have a local band open their shows. The promoter is also responsible for booking this opening act. For the local band, opening for a well-known band can be their big break, a chance to become better-known themselves, particularly when all the tickets have been sold. Playing the opening set of a sold-out concert is an experience that any local band would like to have.

Most bands have a manager, the person who looks after the band's business. In addition to organizing the band's shows, the manager is also responsible for organizing the band's recording schedule.

Track 1.15

Thank you, Larry. Before we finish, I'm sure that you're all wondering how successful the first two legs of the 'Get Shorty' tour were. Well, the accountants down at Thornbank's have finished crunching the numbers, and I think you'll like them.

As you can see from the chart on the screen – and as I'm sure you all remember – the 'Get Shorty' tour lasted a little over three months, and consisted of 44 shows in close to 30 cities. Forty-four shows and 44 sell-outs. Congratulations, boys. You batted a thousand, if you'll permit me a baseball expression.

Anyway, this all translates into a very healthy gross: $147,484,870 worth of gross revenue, to be exact. I'll repeat that number, so you can bask in its limelight. Your gross revenue was $147,484,870. That's not rock music, boys, that's more than the GDP of Kiribati.

If we take a look at the first two shows, in San Diego on March the 28th and 30th, you'll see that the gross was only $29,909,029. That doesn't look like much, but you have to remember that the Sports Arena holds fewer than 15,000 people. So it was a very good beginning. Paul, you asked about New York. The band only played one night in New York City itself, but when you add in the two shows you did across the river in New Jersey, attendance was a very respectable 55,347. When you add up all the shows on the first leg of the tour, a grand total of 499,109 North Americans saw a Short Shrift concert this spring.

Europe was even more profitable, because the stadiums held more people. Over all, more than one million people saw a show in Europe. The biggest show was in Berlin, where the attendance was 70,443. All in all, the average attendance for the European shows was 65,815, and with an average ticket price of 86.54 – that's dollars, not euros – your average gross per European show was $5,695,655. And when you multiply that by 16, well, altogether you grossed $91,130,480. Not bad for a month's work, seeing as how you opened in Belgium on June the 10th and closed in Paris exactly one month later.

Track 1.16

Hello, my name is Janice Sandstrom. I'm grateful to Tony for inviting me here today – and not only because it gets me out of the office for a while! It also gives me a chance to speak to you about managing your band's business. It's odd to look at it like that, isn't it? But that's what it is – a business. A pretty complex business. But you know that already – that's why you're here. I know Tony has already spoken to you about the recording side of the business. I'm going to talk to you about going on the road, about the business of playing concerts. And in particular, I'm going to talk about treating all this as work. We'll talk about finding work, about dealing with employers, and about how to negotiate the terms of your employment. Then if you have any questions, I'll be happy to answer them.

Track 1.17

So, let's start with finding work. Now, I know *work* is a dirty term in the music business, that you all want to be cool and say *gig*, say 'Yeah, we got a gig tonight at the Garden' – but you don't have a gig, you have a job. Let your band members talk about getting gigs. You are business people. You talk about finding work.

So how do business people find work? They talk to people. They do research. They send their CVs out. So the first step is to figure out who you're going to talk to. Business people looking for a job contact potential employers; so should you. Who are your potential employers? Well, there are quite a few of them, actually. There are the club owners in your area, some of whom you probably already know. Contact them. There are local promoters, who might need bands for a show. Contact them, too. Maybe there are groups a little further up in the hierarchy than yours; they might well need an opening act when they come into town. But you won't know unless you talk to them, right? And you might want to contact universities, too. They often put on shows for their students. If you don't take the time to talk to *potential* employers, it's unlikely that you'll find yourself with many *actual* employers.

What sort of research should you do? Organized research. Set up a reliable system where you can track the names of all the people and places, where you can keep track of what shows are going on – where and when they're going on, who's playing – and you need a system that lets you sort this information in different ways. Which clubs have regular music nights on which nights? How often do out-of-town bands come in, and who do they get to play with them? How often does the college down the road put on a concert for its students? How many bands do they normally get? And you can't be passive about gathering this information. You need to check websites every day. You need to go through your local newspapers every day. When was the last time you looked at the university newspaper? Do you even know what it's called?

Organizing all this information sounds like a lot of work … because it is. It's your job now. But you need to be organized if you want to talk to the right people at the right time. Organization is the key to using your time effectively, and the key to keeping your band employed.

Track 1.18

Brendan: I think 'promoter' is one of those job descriptions that everybody has heard of, but maybe you're not quite sure what it is exactly that promoters do.

Isabelle: I think you're right. Well, let's just say that promoters promote. They make sure that people know about, and get people interested in, a particular show.

Brendan: A show? I always thought that promoters promoted bands.

Isabelle: No. Band managers promote bands. Now, obviously, promoters develop good working relationships with bands, and we want the bands to be successful, but promoting the show is the primary thing. The promoter also sets up the show. We're responsible for finding the venue, for making sure that the equipment you need to put on a show – things like the lights and the sound system, even things like security at times – we make sure all those things are in order.

Brendan: I see. How did you get your start in promoting?

Isabelle: I was in college, actually, and I worked part-time for a law firm that represented local bands, and, well, one thing led to another.

Brendan: Did you get your degree?

Isabelle: Yes, I did. I majored in Fine Arts and got my BFA.

Brendan: Do you find the degree helpful in your work?

Isabelle: The degree? Not really, to be honest. But the lawyers I was working for convinced me to take two courses that have been a big help.

Brendan: Mm. What were they?

Isabelle: One was Business Law. I spend a lot of my time working with contracts, and that course laid the foundation. The other was Decisions in History, which sounds like an odd course, but history is filled with terrible decision-making, with people doing what they shouldn't have done and not doing what they should have. You can study those mistakes and figure out how a better decision could have been made. Then apply that realization to today's world and to your own situation. I would really recommend both of these courses to anybody who wants a career in the music industry.

Brendan: What other advice do you have for people who are looking for such a career?

Isabelle: Well, I've been doing this for almost 12 years now, and the main thing for me is taking the time to read the fine print.

Brendan: The fine print? Of a contract?

Isabelle: That's right. So let's say I book your band to play a concert – well, here at the college auditorium. Right?

Brendan: OK.

Isabelle: Well, both of us – the band and I – we need to get paid. And the way we'll probably get paid is through the door split.

Brendan: Er, the door split?

Isabelle: Yes, I'm sorry. 'The door' is basically the money that comes from the tickets that were sold. You see, sometimes, promoters will pay the band a straight fee to play the show, say $2,000. This happens quite a bit when you're opening for another band. The fancy name, by the way, is 'guarantee'. So opening acts get paid one way, but the main acts generally get a percentage of the ticket sales. And the promoter gets the other percentage. Common rates are usually in the 80–20 or 70–30 range.

Brendan: With you getting more?

Isabelle: No, it's generally to the advantage of the band. But the expenses for the show have to be paid for, and sometimes they come off the top and sometimes they come from the promoter's split, so that's why it's really important to go through the contract carefully, and make sure you know what's in it.

Brendan: Thank you for an interesting conversation.

Isabelle: My pleasure.

Katherine: So, Rodney, can you tell us how you got interested in Woodstock?

Rodney: Well, basically, even though I grew up in Australia, I was born in Sullivan County, New York – not too far from Bethel.

Katherine: Bethel? Bethel, New York?

Rodney: Right, so seeing as I was born right where it happened, so to speak, it seemed natural that, you know, when it came time to do my dissertation in Contemporary History, well, it just seemed natural that I would concentrate on Woodstock.

Katherine: I'm a little confused, Rodney. Is Bethel near Woodstock?

Rodney: No, not really. Bethel and Woodstock are both in upstate New York, of course, but New York is a pretty big state, and they're about 55 miles apart, a little bit more.

Katherine: So what's the connection between Bethel and Woodstock?

Rodney: Oh, I see. Well, OK, let's start at the beginning, then. Ah, Woodstock – or, to be more precise, 'Woodstock Music and Art Fair: An Aquarian exposition: three days of peace and music' – was not held in the town of Woodstock, New York. It was held in the town of Bethel. Of course, in the end, the festival didn't last three days, either. It went on through to Monday, so it wound up being, you know, three-and-a-half days of peace and music.

Katherine: Really? So is there a big concert site in Bethel?

Rodney: No, not really. Woodstock took place on 600 acres of Max Yasgur's dairy farm.

Katherine: Max— I'm sorry, what was the last name?

Rodney: Yasgur – Y-A-S-G-U-R.

Katherine: So how did the most famous concert in history wind up miles away from the town it was named for on a 600-acre dairy farm owned by a guy named Max Yasgur?

Rodney: Well, the story begins down in New York City, where two young men, John Roberts and Joel Rosenman, placed an ad in the *Wall Street Journal* and *New York Times* announcing that they were 'Young men with unlimited capital looking for interesting, legitimate investment opportunities and business propositions'. You need to remember this when you think about Woodstock – its genesis was two guys advertising in the *New York Times* and *Wall Street Journal*. Woodstock began as business, not revolution. Anyway, about 5,000 people responded to the ad, including – perhaps – two men working in the music industry: Michael Lang and Artie Kornfeld.

Katherine: Lang, L-A-N-G?

Rodney: That's right. Anyway, Lang and Kornfeld had developed some ideas about building a recording studio in Woodstock – where Bob Dylan and some other rock artists were living – and they thought that a music festival would be a good way to promote it. I said *perhaps* about Kornfeld and Lang responding to the ad, because Kornfeld has always maintained that a lawyer referred them to Roberts and Rosenman. In any event, the four eventually decided to form the Woodstock Ventures partnership. And during their meetings and brainstorming sessions, the focus of the plan moved from the recording studio to the music festival.

Katherine: You mentioned Bob Dylan. Was he at Woodstock?

Rodney: Woodstock, the town – not Woodstock, the concert. You see, Woodstock was a kind of artist's colony, and a few rock stars had moved up there. But anyway, in April 1969, Woodstock Ventures managed to sign Creedence Clearwater Revival to play – they were the first artists to sign and they got $10,000, which was pretty good money in those days. And, well, after that, more and more artists started to say 'yes', and the concert took on a life of its own.

Katherine: It sounds like the promoters were really generous.

Rodney: No, not really. Their business plan – though that's probably a term that overstates the organization of the festival – the model was to offer more money than the artists were used to getting. So while they actually sold 186,000 tickets to the festival and collected about $1.3 million in advance sales, they had only estimated costs at $500,000, when in fact their costs ran to $2.6 million.

Katherine: They actually sold 186,000 tickets? I thought Woodstock was a free concert.

Rodney: Yeah, one of my favourite stats about Woodstock is that 4,062 people actually got refunds on their tickets, because they were never able to get into the concert, because of all the other people. The decision to make it a free concert wasn't made until Thursday August the 14th – the night before the festival was scheduled to begin.

Katherine: Fascinating. So did they lose a lot of money on Woodstock?

Rodney: Yes and no. In the short term, things were not good. By the end of the festival, Woodstock Ventures was about $1.3 million in debt.

Katherine: So it *was* a bad investment!

Rodney: Well, the festival itself was a bad investment, I guess, but with the Woodstock movie, Woodstock albums and Woodstock merchandising, it did make a profit in the end.

Katherine: So the partners got rich?

Rodney: I'm not so sure about that – at least not rich from Woodstock. About six weeks after the festival, Rosenman and Roberts bought out Lang and Kornfeld for $31,240 each.

Katherine: Right. We only have a few minutes left. Um, is there something you can tell us about the concerts themselves?

Rodney: I think the most important thing to remember is how confusing the scene was. The acts needed helicopters – including army helicopters – to get to the festival site. The concert was supposed to start Friday at 4 p.m., but most of the acts couldn't get there. Richie Havens was about the only performer already there, so he opened the festival – at 5.07 p.m. – and played for close to three hours before the other acts showed up. Every time he tried to finish his set, they told him to keep playing.

Katherine: Wow. So how many acts were there at Woodstock?

Rodney: There were 32 acts scheduled, but one of them – Iron Butterfly – never made it.

Katherine: Sorry, who never made it?

Rodney: Iron Butterfly was the name of the band. People probably don't remember them now, but they were big in '69. They didn't make it because they were stuck in a Manhattan heliport. Jimi Hendrix was supposed to close the concert Sunday evening, but by that time it was running nine hours late, so he wound up playing Monday morning.

Katherine: Does anybody know how many people actually showed up for the festival?

Rodney: Not with any precision. One of the famous announcements from the stage was about serving breakfast in bed for 400,000, and that seems to be a popular number. The official estimates range anywhere from 150,000 to 700,000, with 400 to 500,000 being the consensus.

Katherine: This is really fascinating. Can you give us one final fact that you like about Woodstock?

Rodney: Well, I think Woodstock is fascinating because of the tension between this hippy ideal, with kids skinny-dipping in the ponds and free music and all that, with the business and organizational side. A favourite fact? Well, let me leave you with two numbers. The first is 600 – which is the number of portable toilets at the site. Think about sharing a toilet with 1,000 people for three days. Um, they forgot to bring in any trash cans, too, by the way. And the other number is three – which is how many people died. And that's an incredibly small number given the number of people who were there, the amount of drugs they took, and the fact that the organizers really weren't prepared for it.

Katherine: Dr Rodney Paltz, thank you so much for your time.

UNIT 3

Track 1.20

1 Originally, I wanted to be an Earth scientist, and in fact that's what I studied as an undergraduate. But one thing led to another, and I spent the summer after I graduated law school camping all over the American West. I thought to myself, there has to be a way I can combine my love of nature, my knowledge of how nature works, and my law degree. Fortunately, there was.

Track 1.21

2 I was more interested in real property and land law when I was in law school, to be honest. But the law firm where I found my first job had a small department that handled things like improper dismissals and safety issues in the workplace, and I found that I quite liked the work.

Track 1.22

3 My family arrived in Canada when I was 13. It took me some time to adjust, I must admit, but I eventually graduated from law school six years ago. I wasn't sure what I was going to do when I graduated, but my first client was a friend of the family's who had been arrested, and I defended him. Then he had a friend who had also been arrested, and she had a friend who was charged with quite a serious crime, and my practice just continued to grow.

Track 1.23

4 I've always loved the water, you see. And so when I went to law school and found out that there was a whole body of law that focuses on what happens when you leave dry

land, well, I knew that that was the field I wanted to work in. And I've never looked back.

Track 1.24

5 It's quite a broad area of law, isn't it? Perhaps that's why I like it. I can spend Monday working on a bankruptcy, Tuesday protecting my clients' copyrights, and the rest of the week finalizing a merger between two firms.

Track 1.25

Arthur: So, Ms Nicholson asked me to stop by to talk to you to about Civics. Do you study Civics at school where you come from?

Student 1: I'm sorry, what does it mean, 'Civics'?

Arthur: I see. Right, well, Civics is basically the study of what being a good citizen means. You learn how government works, what your duties as a citizen are, and what rights you have. So, for example, just yesterday I gave my students an exam on how our laws become laws.

Student 1: Thank you.

Ms Nicholson: Arthur, I think it would be very instructive for us to hear more about laws becoming laws.

Arthur: Sure. Well, we start with a Bill, which is simply a proposed law. First, we have the consultation phase, which is where the lawmakers decide what exactly is going to be in the Bill. Before the Bill is even written down, a Green Paper or a White Paper is published, and this allows public involvement and gives people the chance to comment on the Bill.

Student 2: Is there a difference?

Arthur: Between …?

Student 2: Between the Green Paper and the White Paper.

Arthur: Oh, I see. There is, actually. But it doesn't really matter to us. Well, then, after the consultation phase, the next step is to introduce the Bill to Parliament, and this is called the First Reading, though the Bill isn't really in published form at this stage.

Student 2: Is it in electronic form?

Arthur: That's a good question. No, it's not, so there's really not much to read until the Second Reading, which is when Parliament actually sees the Bill, and gets to discuss it and debate it. After that, the Bill goes to the Committee Phase of the process, where it's examined by what we call a Standing Committee – though, of course, chairs are provided.

Student 1: Excuse me? I don't understand.

Arthur: It was just a joke. I'm sorry if I confused you. So, as I was saying, the Bill goes to committee, where it is examined and often changed and amended. Then the committee sends the revised Bill to the whole Parliament for the Report Stage, which is where the Bill is actually voted on, and then its Third Reading.

Student 1: So there are three readings in all?

Arthur: Yes, but keep in mind that here in the UK, we have two Houses – the House of Commons and the House of Lords – so after the Bill is done in one house – usually the Commons, but not necessarily – it moves over to the other House.

Student 2: And do they do the same thing?

Arthur: More or less. Well, once the Bill has passed both houses, it's ready for the Royal Assent.

Student 2: Er, Royal what?

Arthur: Assent. It means 'approval'. The UK is a monarchy after all, and so it's the Queen, or King, that officially makes a law. Now, technically, the monarch here in the UK can withhold assent, but the last time that happened was in 1708, so this is very much a formality. By the way, the Assent is given in old French, *La Reyne le veult* – or *Le Roy* if there is a king. Isn't it nice to think that William the Conqueror remains influential even in the 21st century? Anyway, once you have the Royal Assent, your Bill has turned into an Act of Parliament.

Ms Nicholson: Thank you, Arthur, for that fascinating explanation. Are there any questions?

Track 1.26

In one sense, there are at least as many legal systems in the world as there are countries. I say 'at least' because in many countries, there's more than one operative legal system. Be that as it may, all of those various legal systems are usually based on common law, civil law or religious law – and often they're based on more than one. Even totalitarian regimes will usually base their legal system on elements of civil or religious law. So in a way, there are only three primary legal systems in the world today. There are other approaches to law, to be sure. But even approaches like socialist law, which was used in most Communist countries, was adapted from the starting point of civil law, and older approaches like customary law are often reflected in our three approaches.

Before I go any further, let me clarify what I mean by 'religious law'. I'm referring to systems like Roman Catholic canon law and Muslim Sharia – systems that are based not only on 'God', in a broad sense, but that also embody some moral sense, some sense of how people ought to act.

Track 1.27

Now, when we talk about civil law, what exactly do we mean? Well, the overriding element of civil law is that legislation is the fundamental source of law, and that citizens have the right to a written body of law, and that they can easily get access to that written body. That's what we mean when we talk of 'codified' law.

Not all legal systems rely on legislation for laws. Later on, we'll talk in some detail about how the other legal approaches look at the fundamental source of law. For now, let me just point out that in common law, the basis – at least in theory – is judges' decisions.

But, let's stay with civil law. Civil law dates back to the end of the Roman Empire. In fact, civil law is sometimes called 'Roman law', though that's wrong. As we will see, Roman law is really only one element in civil law. Anyway, the Roman Emperor Justinian I issued his Justinian Codes in the sixth century – that's AD, in case you're wondering. There were four parts to the codes, and all four had the force of law. And so, in effect, the Justinian Codes were huge collections of all the laws of the land.

Track 1.28

Here's a question for us to start with today: How many countries are there?

According to the website of the United States State Department, there are 194 independent states in the world. But when I looked on another website, it said that there were 206 sovereign states. And when I checked with the United Nations, there were 193 members. Other sites said 195 countries. What's going on? Is the number 193 or is it 206? Basically, the problem is not that people don't know how to count, it's that different people are counting different things. And the reason they're counting different things is that they're using different definitions.

So, this is the first thing we're going to talk about today: clear definitions of the words *country*, *nation* and *state*. Because if we don't have clear definitions of these three words, we're going to get very confused later on.

So, let's start by establishing that, for our purposes, *country* is going to refer to the land, the territory inside the borders of our independent entity. Now, not everybody uses the word *country* in this way, but that's OK: as long as we're consistent in our use of it, we won't be confused.

Next, we're going to use *nation* to refer to a group of people who share some common characteristics, characteristics like history, ethnic origin and also language. Now, this is a problematic category because it's so politically abstract. Canadians share a common ethnic origin and a common language with many Americans. Do we really want to say they represent just one nation? Just how many common traits do you need to have a nation?

So our starting question was wrong: it's not 'How many countries are there?' or even 'How many nations are there?'. The question we really want to answer today is 'How many sovereign states are there?', and by *state* we mean two things. Firstly, it refers to a government that exerts control over its territory, or at least part of its territory, and also that territory's population. Secondly, it means that the territory and its population are not reliant on an outside power.

But now things get *more* complicated. I've given you my definition of *state*, but my definition is not *the* definition. There is no *the* definition. There are schools of thought. Isn't that wonderful? This is the most basic question in international law, this 'What makes *you* international?', and the answer is 'It depends'.

You didn't come here today to hear 'It depends', I know. But you see, international law is like a big club – a club of sovereign states, to use our terminology – and if you want to understand a club, then you need some idea of how that club chooses its members. And how it keeps people it doesn't want to be members out of the club.

So let's look at these two schools of thought, known as the 'constitutive' school and the 'declarative' school, and how they decide who gets to be a sovereign state.

Track 1.29

1 The committee is trying to put the rules for becoming a member into a code.
2 The enforcement of the decision is necessary if we want to be taken seriously.
3 Our independence is unobtainable unless we keep working to meet the criteria outlined in the Montevideo convention.
4 There is absolutely no justification for the publication of another Home Office study on why prisoners want to get out of jail.
5 What is the legality of gambling in your country?
6 In the USA, Congress has the power to pass legislation.
7 There is no relevance in this situation to the Treaty of St Germain.
8 The establishment of a newly sovereign state is always an important event.

Track 1.30

Student: Good morning, Professor Holmes. May I come in?

Professor Holmes: Of course. How can I help you?

Student: I'm Oliver Aletas. I'm a student in your Business Law course.

Professor Holmes: I see.

Student: Yes. You see, I've decided to come back to university, but of course it's been a long time since I was a student, and it's not so easy to remember how to be a good student.

Professor Holmes: Yes, it can take a while to get back in the swing of things. So, are you having difficulty with anything in particular?

Student: Well, yes, as a matter of fact. I know that you gave a big lecture on how common law works, but, well, I'm still rather confused by it.

Professor Holmes: Hm. Well, I want to ask you a question, but I don't want you to give me an answer just yet. OK?

Student: OK.

Professor Holmes: The question is, 'Where do laws come from?'

Student: Where do laws come from.

Professor Holmes: In a sense, this is a very easy question to answer, but in a sense it's also a very philosophical one. I'll leave the philosophic side of the question to the Philosophy Department for today, and just say that the easy answer is that laws come from the government.

Student: OK. But isn't that true for every system of law, not just common law?

Professor Holmes: Yes, it is. Now, let's imagine a country that doesn't have a very strong central government. You might say that if the government is weak, then there won't be laws, but really what winds up happening, over time, is that there are laws, but the laws are local laws. So if we're in England, well, there will be one set of laws that are obeyed in London, and there will be another set of laws in Liverpool, and another set in Bristol, and so forth. And sometimes the laws will be similar, but other times different localities might deal with the same problem in very different ways.

Student: So for example, a thief might be executed in Bristol, but only put in jail in London?

Professor Holmes: That's right, though to be honest the focus here is more on how local laws handle business and property disputes, not crimes.

Student: OK.

Professor Holmes: Now, imagine that you become head of this not-very-strong government in England, and you want to make it stronger. You're the king, in other words. If you want to make it stronger, well obviously you need it to have more authority, right? Now one very important area of authority for any government is the area of law. But people aren't really obeying *your* law. You have the people in London obeying London law and the people in Liverpool obeying Liverpool law and so on, but what you want is to have all those people obeying your law, obeying the same law. You see?

Student: I think so. And was this really the situation in England?

Professor Holmes: Basically. So, starting in around the 12th century, English kings started to assert their authority and send judges out around the country to hear cases under the king's law, rather than local law.

And after a while, because all these king's judges were applying the same law – the king's law – the cases started to be decided in more or less the same way, in a way that was common throughout England.

Student: Common law.

Professor Holmes: That's right. Now, think about this process in a little more detail. Let's pretend that I'm a medieval judge and the king sends me out to Liverpool and another judge out to Cornwall and another one out to – I don't know – Leeds, and this is the Middle Ages, so we're gone for a while. Maybe even a few months. But eventually, we all come back to the king in London and we give him a report about the cases we heard and what we decided. And there are times when we also give the king some explanation of how we reached that decision. Particularly when the case has some new element to it.

Student: Mm. This has something to do with setting a precedent, doesn't it?

Professor Holmes: Excellent, Oliver. I think you may understand more than you think you do.

Student: But how does precedent work?

Professor Holmes: Well, I was in Cornwall when I heard my case, but let's say that some time later the judge who goes to Leeds hears a similar case.

Student: OK.

Professor Holmes: Well, let's say that we judges all read the other judges' reports. The ones where they explained their decisions to the king. Now, when the judge in Leeds hears this similar case, he's going to say to himself, 'Hm, Holmes heard something similar and reached this certain conclusion. I should probably do likewise.' And if enough cases are similar enough, and enough other colleagues hear them, eventually we have a system of precedence, where the decisions that were made yesterday help determine the decisions we need to make today.

Student: Yes, but what if the judge in Leeds disagrees with your decision?

Professor Holmes: Excellent question, Oliver. Well, of course, sometimes I think that a decision is incorrect, and so I reach another decision.

Student: So how do we know which decision is the right one?

Professor Holmes: Another excellent question. Well, if we were all equal colleagues, I guess the people who agreed with me would follow my example, and the people who agreed with the other would follow his example …

Student: … and pretty soon you wouldn't have a common law any more.

Professor Holmes: … and pretty soon you wouldn't have a common law any more. But, we aren't all equal. The king is above us. And so …

Student: And so the king decides which decision to follow …

Professor Holmes: … and you, me and all our other colleagues have to follow the king's decision. And that, Oliver, is the concept of *Stare Decisis*, the concept of binding precedent.

Student: And is that really what common law is?

Professor Holmes: More or less. Life in the 21st century is a bit more complex than life in the 12th, so instead of having the king decide which decision is the right decision, we have a series of different courts, but the same reasoning applies: the courts are not all equal, there is a hierarchy, and when a court at one level reaches a decision, the courts at the levels below have to follow it.

Student: I see.

Professor Holmes: Let me stress, too, that this system of common law took centuries to develop, and it certainly wasn't something that some person set out to create. It was created, truly, one decision at a time. And that took a lot of time.

Student: OK, Professor Holmes, thank you. You've helped me out quite a bit.

CONSOLIDATION 1

Track 2.1

The media play an important role in keeping people informed and entertained. In the second half of the 20th century, newspapers, radio and television dominated the media world, but in the 21st century, the Internet has disrupted their position. Television broadcasts are no longer the only way to view a television show; people can read the daily newspaper without subscribing to it or buying it at a news-stand; radio talk shows are streamed onto computers rather than received by transistor radios. As a result, the traditional mass media have seen their revenues fall; many struggle just to break even. Television networks, newspapers, even radio stations have begun to put their content behind paywalls, asking consumers to pay for something that they often think should be free. At the same time, internet service providers are under pressure from media companies to restrict their customers' ability to access illegal content.

Track 2.2

Richard: I'd like to start by thanking you and Professor Hoffman for inviting me to join your class today. In a few minutes, we'll start working on some case studies, but first I'd like to address a question that Professor Hoffman alluded to a few minutes ago: In the age of the Internet, does it make sense to invest in newspapers? In a word, 'no'. And I think it's instructive to walk through why not. So first of all, let's start with a premise, and that is that investors invest in a company when they think the company will be profitable. And to decide whether a company will be profitable, you have to look first at how it makes its money. How do newspapers make money? That's not a rhetorical question. Does anybody know?

Student 1: Advertising.

Richard: Advertising. Right. That's one.

Student 2: Sales?

Richard: 'Sales' is an interesting answer. How do newspapers sell their products?

Student 2: I don't know, at news-stands?

Richard: Uh-huh. Any other ways?

Student 3: To subscribers?

Richard: Right. News-stand sales plus subscriptions is known as a newspaper's readership, by the way. Now, it turns out that newspapers don't make much money on readership. In fact, they often lose money on subscriptions, and maybe make a little on news-stand sales. Traditionally, newspapers have made their money through advertising.

So here, from an investor's point of view, we have a

complication. As an investor, I like it when the company makes money on its core product. But with newspapers, if you're really lucky, you'll break even on actually selling your product, so the only way for you to be profitable is to be a delivery system for the advertising.

Now, how much money you can charge for advertising is a direct consequence of how many people are reading your newspaper. So, if I'm thinking about investing in a newspaper in the age of the Internet, my question becomes: What has the Internet done to your readership? Well, let's see. Ten or 11 years ago, there were 1,489 daily newspapers, and they had a total circulation – which is a measure of readership – of 56,182,635. That's a lot of newspapers. Last year, though, there were 1,408 daily newspapers, and they had a total circulation of roughly 48.6 million. That's a 13.5% decline, which is not insubstantial. On the other hand, a lot of people are still reading newspapers.

But what about advertising? Well, here the numbers are pretty ugly. Just in the last year, advertising revenues for the industry were down 16.6%, to $37.85 billion, which also includes classified ads, like real-estate ads, used-car sales and people selling their old refrigerators and other household appliances. What's especially worrying is that print-ad revenues have declined for 16 straight quarters. So we have an industry that doesn't make money directly from selling its primary product, it's selling less of that product, and its primary source of revenue seems to be locked into a decline. That's not the working definition of a healthy industry.

Student 2: I'm sorry, Mr Wexler, but what about online newspapers?

Richard: That's an excellent question. Can newspapers switch their product from newsprint to the Internet and do well there? The problem is that no one knows yet if there is a sustainable business model. Even online, where are newspapers going to get their money? The same places as they get their money now, through advertising or through selling their content.

Now, a lot of people visit newspaper websites every day. Last month, there were 69,125,573 unique visits to newspaper websites. And those websites generated a fair amount of ad revenue: just over $27.5 million last quarter. So that sounds like a fair amount of money, except for the fact that it represents an 11.8% decline from the previous quarter, and isn't, in any event, enough to make up for the losses the newspapers are seeing on the print side.

As for selling the content, we see more and more newspapers putting their content behind a paywall, saying, listen, we can't afford to give our product away. Information may want to be free, but journalists like to eat. Will that work? It's too soon to tell. But in a recent poll of online newspaper readers, only about 23% indicated that they would be willing to pay to read a newspaper online, so if it's going to work, some attitudes will have to change.

Now, am I saying that the 21st century will be the end of newspapers? No, not necessarily. What I am saying is that the old business model is on its way out, and there is, as yet, no convincing new business model to take its place. And so for now, this investor will be investing in other areas.

Track 2.3

The term 'mass media' was first used in the 1920s to describe the rise of radio broadcasts and the increase in the circulation of newspapers and magazines. The key to the term is that these media are designed to reach a large audience.

Duplication of material is what makes mass media possible. And while the term was initially used to describe radio and newspapers, it was actually Johannes Gutenberg's printing press that opened the way to mass media in the 15th century.

In the 20th century, the reach of the mass media expanded dramatically. The cost of duplicating materials declined, and new technologies like television and film allowed the mass media to reach an even wider audience.

In the 21st century, the Internet seems ready to overtake the traditional mass media. Not only does it offer new ways to distribute information and entertainment, like radio and newspapers, it also offers new forms of mass media, such as blogs and podcasts. With its tremendous audience (currently estimated at 1.9 billion people worldwide), the Internet can drastically increase a medium's potential audience. On the other hand, the fact that materials can easily be duplicated and delivered on the Internet, plus the fact that the Internet encourages the unbundling of the traditional packaging of mass-media content (paying to read a single article in a magazine, for example, rather than paying for the entire magazine, or buying a song rather than the entire CD) means that the traditional media companies will have to alter their business model if they want to survive in the Internet age.

Track 2.4

Interviewer: I'd like to ask Dr Haskell to join us back on stage. Dr Haskell, you were saying before that, as a television historian, you don't think TV is necessarily a thing of the past.

Dr Haskell: That's right, though I think I should explain right away that I think television faces a number of immediate challenges if it's going to continue to be a relevant media source in the 21st century.

Interviewer: Why don't we look at some of those challenges, then. I presume that the Internet is number one on the list.

Dr Haskell: No, not necessarily. What I mean by that is that the amazing growth of the Internet as an entertainment medium and a news-gathering medium has certainly altered the way that television has to do business. At the same time, television is certainly capable of competing with the Internet, or – better, much better – is certainly capable of coexisting with the Internet.

Interviewer: That's an interesting distinction. Can I ask you to elaborate?

Dr Haskell: Well, it's always interesting to see how language shades our conception of something out there in the world. So here we have a household appliance, something that once upon a time only came in black and white, and had rabbit-ear antennas, and now it's in 3D and has a digital decoder or a satellite dish out on the balcony or whatever. And that appliance we call a 'television'. And then we have the content, what comes out of that appliance when we turn it on, and that, too, is called 'television'. And so those two things – the appliance and the content – tend to conflate.

But we can put the appliance to one side because it's already changed quite a lot in its history, and we still consider it a television set. They may call them home theatres in the stores, but everybody knows that it's a big plasma-screen TV, not a small plasma-screen cinema.

Interviewer: So if tomorrow the signal comes through broadband and not the satellite dish, or if the screen is also used to work your computer …

Dr Haskell: … then I'm pretty confident that we'll be asking people to turn the TV on so we can watch it, and not the computer. If the content of the television set comes through the Internet, I don't think that one fact will change our relationship to television.

Interviewer: So what is the biggest challenge to television?

Dr Haskell: Content. The big problem with content is that it costs money to make it. A lot of money. Just to put this in some kind of perspective, if the BBC decides to develop a new drama series, the projection works out to be between five hundred and seven hundred thousand pounds per hour. Or here's another: the pilot programme for the American TV series *Lost* cost $11.5 million. That's for one two-hour episode. And they weren't even sure it would be a hit.

Interviewer: So where does all that money come from?

Dr Haskell: And here we come to the heart of the matter. In television, the broadcasters basically have three ways to generate money. One is advertising, the second is viewing fees, and the third, for government-owned broadcasters, is some sort of TV tax.

Each of these is problematic for television in the 21st century. Let's start with advertising. Now, advertising can still generate a lot of money, particularly for a hit show. In fact, when *Lost* aired its final episode, 30-second spots cost $900,000.

However, ad revenues are in decline, both because television viewership for traditional broadcasters is in decline, and because there is more competition. Companies usually have an overall advertising budget, and if they decide to spend some of that money on internet advertising, for instance, that means that much less money will be spent on TV.

Interviewer: So that leaves viewing fees and TV taxes.

Dr Haskell: And there's no way a government can charge its citizens enough money to generate high-quality content.

Interviewer: What about viewing fees?

Dr Haskell: Here I'm a bit more confident. When you look at broadcasters that charge fees for their content – cable and satellite broadcasters, say – you see that they have a good, stable source of revenue. The simple truth is that people are lazy, and once they sign up for a service like cable or satellite TV, they usually keep it.

Interviewer: You make it sound like the future of television rests on people's laziness.

Dr Haskell: In a way it does.

Interviewer: In your writings, you make a point of the cultural aspects of television. How does that fit into the future of television?

Dr Haskell: Well, people like to share cultural events, and television falls into that category. It's entertainment, yes, but it's also a social activity in the way that watching a YouTube video isn't. And, as a result, we gather around the television to watch important events. You know,

back in 1968, there was a presidential election in the United States, and this was the time of the Vietnam War. The Democrats held their convention in Chicago, and there were huge protests, and battles between the protestors and the police, and at one point the police charged the protestors, and the protestors were chanting 'The whole world is watching', and that was the power of television back then because people were watching and those scenes helped Richard Nixon, the Republican candidate, get into the White House.

'The whole world is watching' is more true today than ever. Seven hundred million people, maybe more, will tune in to watch a World Cup final. Two billion people are presumed to have watched Princess Diana's funeral. Television makes us feel like we're a part of something, even if we're sitting in our living rooms.

Interviewer: So we will keep watching television because it makes us feel closer to other people?

Dr Haskell: Yes. And also, I think, because television will figure out how to keep us watching. Television has learned from what happened to music and newspapers, and it's working on ways to treat the Internet as a distribution network, and not just as a threat. And that's what I mean by coexistence.

Interviewer: Dr Haskell, thank you very much for sharing your thoughts with us.

Note: Track 2.5 relates to the photocopiable activity for Consolidation 1; the audio transcript for it appears in the Teacher's Book (page 34).

UNIT 4

Track 2.6

How will the world end? Will aliens attack us just like in *Independence Day*? Will the Sun die and burn us to a crisp? No one is sure, but we do know that the universe *is* trying to kill us. Phil Plait, a noted astronomer, has calculated the odds for a number of galactic endings. Here are some of the ways we all could go, and their probabilities.

Let's start with solar flares. They probably won't kill anybody, but they could cause all our electrical power grids to collapse, and deplete the ozone layer. We can't do anything to prevent solar flares, but we can lessen their impact through planning.

Next on our list is an asteroid hitting us. If a small asteroid hits, then any damage would be localized, but big asteroids can cause damage on a global scale. Asteroids can be deadly, particularly if they land on your head, and the chances of dying from an asteroid impact are one in 732,600. If we have enough advance warning, and we can launch a rocket, then we can blow up a threatening asteroid, or at least push it out of the way.

Could the Sun become a supernova? Probably not, but in theory it could. It would destroy the ozone layer, flood the Earth with radiation and generally cause a lot of unhappiness. The odds of it happening to you? Approximately one in ten million. We can't prevent it, but we shouldn't spend much time worrying about it.

What about another type of solar event, a gamma-ray burst? Well, that would be bad, because it would set the Earth on fire, and we would all burn to death. It's not very likely, though; the odds are only about one in 14 million.

Which is good, since we couldn't prevent it.

What about black holes? Could we be sucked into a black hole and spend the rest of our days like Alice in Wonderland? Probably not in our (or anybody else's) lifetimes. The likelihood is somewhere around one in one trillion (that's a one followed by 12 zeros). Good thing, too, because while we might not know what exists on the other side of a black hole, we do know that nothing could survive the journey through. And we also know of no way to stop it from happening.

Now, on to Martians and other aliens …

Track 2.7

Now, on to Martians and other aliens. Of course, we can't say how probable it is that aliens are a threat to our existence, given that there isn't any undeniable evidence that aliens even exist. What I can say is that in 1995, we only knew of three exoplanets – and by that I mean planets outside our solar system. But at the last count, we were up to 716, and I'm sure that number will continue to rise. But since we don't know for certain that aliens are out there, there's no way for us to calculate the probabilities. So the answer to the question of 'What are my chances of dying in an alien attack?' is a big 'Not given'. And I'll leave it to you to decide whether that's better or worse than one in a trillion. On the other hand, we could prevent an alien attack under the right conditions, so that's something in our favour.

Track 2.8

1 When I was on the beach near Rome, I found a coin that dates back to 36 AD.
2 What does this abbreviation 'LAT' mean on the map?
3 If you don't want to keep typing out the word, you can just use 'ORIG'.
4 Why is 'FWKO' an abbreviation used in the oil industry?
5 We don't pronounce the letters 'A-N-Z-A-C' – we say 'ANZAC'.
6 Andrew Cuomo served as HUD Secretary under President Clinton.
7 I used to go swimming at the YWHA pool on 14th Street.
8 Where does the abbreviation 'REM' come from?
9 My postgraduate degree is technically an MJur, but I just say I went to law school.
10 My friend texted me with the abbreviation 'ROTFL', and I have no idea what it means.

Track 2.9

Of all the possible disasters for humankind, one of the most probable comes from Mother Nature: a global epidemic. The last time we had a true global epidemic was in 1918, when a Spanish Flu epidemic killed at least 20 million people. In the 14th century, the Black Death, which was a bubonic-plague epidemic, is estimated to have killed one-third of the European population. Humans have been battling germs for as long as we've been on the planet, and it's clear that sometimes the germs get the upper hand. People tend to think that epidemics are a thing of the past, but people still die of the bubonic plague today; AIDS is still an ongoing threat, and quote-unquote newer diseases like Ebola have the potential to explode out of their contained areas.

Perhaps the worst possibility is that a disease that we already have medicine for mutates and becomes resistant. This happens all the time, mostly because antibiotics of all types are way overused, with new strains of diseases like cholera and tuberculosis becoming more problematic. My candidate for the disease most likely to wipe us off the face of the Earth? Staph. Staph infections are caused by bacteria, and there are about 30 different staph bacteria that can infect the human body. Most staph infections are relatively innocuous, but there are some nasty ones, too, that can be fatal. What's more, some of the bacteria have become very resistant to antibiotics. All you need is for one of these bacteria to mutate, to become a bit more virulent, a bit more contagious and a bit more resistant to the remaining antibiotics, and it could spread around the world long before we develop an effective antibiotic. Roughly 12,000 years ago, there was a huge die-off of mammals in the western hemisphere, and one of the leading candidates for why it happened is the outbreak of a virulent disease. Staph might just make people the next woolly rhinoceros.

Track 2.10

World War I began in August 1914, and by the time it ended in November 1918, roughly 16 million people had been killed by the war. By contrast, an estimated 20 million plus people died during the Spanish Flu epidemic, which began in March of 1918 and lasted until June 1920. It's difficult to overstate the effects of the epidemic. Globally, the death rate is estimated to have been as high as 3% of all humans. Matters were made worse by the fact that adults aged 20 to 40 were particularly susceptible to the disease. This is unusual, because the people most at risk of dying from the flu are normally the very young and the very old. For obvious reasons, the majority of military deaths in World War I affected the same age group. The combination of war and epidemic lowered life expectancy dramatically. In the United States, it fell by more than ten years.

The Spanish Flu doesn't belong solely to the past. In 2005, researchers managed to determine the flu's genetic sequence, and in 2007, monkeys were infected with the re-created flu. Let's hope that humans are better prepared to face the Spanish Flu if it makes a comeback.

Track 2.11

But what would happen if our solar system came into contact with a black hole? Few scientists take the chances of this happening very seriously, but scientists do estimate that there are about ten million dead stars in the Milky Way alone, and dead stars are the building blocks of black holes.

Track 2.12

Not every dead star becomes a black hole, of course, but some of them do; in particular, those stars with more than 20 times the mass of our Sun do. Some scientists estimate that there may be hundreds of black holes in our galaxy.

Track 2.13

Most should be in orbit around the centre of the galaxy, and in fact, current theory holds that the galaxy itself is orbiting a massive black hole. But space is a violent place, and some of the smaller black holes could be flung out of the centre. And the theory also holds that once these black holes are no longer orbiting the centre of the galaxy, they can roam throughout the galaxy, a bit like asteroids in our solar system.

Given the size of our galaxy, the likelihood that the Earth will actually run into one of these rogue black holes, as they're called, is quite small. But a black hole doesn't have to hit Earth to make life here very uncomfortable. If it comes close – and close astronomically speaking is about a billion miles – then its gravitational pull could change our planet's orbit, which could lead to extreme changes in temperature, and the end of human life on Earth.

Track 2.14

Rhonda: So, one of Faber's most popular courses is Earth Science 312, which most students know as Armageddon 101. Can you tell us something about the course?

Alma: Well, you know, I find it very interesting how so many students get wrapped up in the Mother Earth/Gaia thing, how they see the Earth as just perfect for life. I certainly want my students to respect the Earth and not abuse it, but I think that respect should be clear-eyed, not mystical. The Earth is not all that nurturing. Approximately 99% of all the species that have ever existed on Earth have become extinct. Ninety-nine per cent!

Rhonda: Not a good track record.

Alma: Not at all. And even today, right now, the Earth would gladly see you dead. For about 75% of the Earth, if you are there without special clothing and instruments, you are dead within 20 minutes or so. And that's not to mention all the special ways Earth has of killing you: the volcanoes, the floods, the earthquakes, etc.

Rhonda: So are you saying that Earth is not good for life?

Alma: No. I'm saying that life has to struggle to survive on Earth, and it's wise not to lose sight of this fact.

Rhonda: One of the highlights of ES312 is your annual 'Top Ten Ways Humanity Could Die' list. What's on the list this year?

Alma: Well, this is a list I put together every year, and it's a list of unexpected ways humanity could be wiped out within the next 100 years. So, for example, one of the things on the list this year is the ecosystem collapsing.

Rhonda: What do you mean?

Alma: Well, the ecosystem is basically the relationships between all the living organisms in a given area. And what's important to remember is that every living organism – because of those relationships – has an effect on every other living organism. Now, living organisms come and go all the time, of course, and ecosystems are usually viable enough that those comings and goings don't really change the ecosystem all that much, but it's possible that so many organisms can come and go that it pushes the ecosystem out of balance, and that causes the ecosystem to collapse.

Rhonda: So what could happen to unbalance the human ecosystem?

Alma: Well, we're living in a time of mass extinction. You may not realize it, but species are dying off at a very fast rate. It's been estimated that just in the tropical rainforests, more than 25,000 species could be becoming extinct … per year. Now, obviously most of those species are things like bacteria and fungi, with some insects and plants, but the thing is that the relationships in an ecosystem are tremendously complex, and one of those

insects might just be the marginal insect, pollinating the marginal plant, and if they go, it could alter the balance in the ecosystem enough to make the ecosystem unviable. And if the tropical rainforests go, that could change the Earth's atmosphere enough to make the air unbreathable for humans.

Rhonda: Oh my!

Alma: Another way the Earth could kill us off is by a reversal of its magnetic field.

Rhonda: Does that happen often?

Alma: About every three hundred thousand years or so. No one is really sure why it happens, but basically the magnetic north pole goes south, and the magnetic south pole goes north. That in itself won't kill us off. But while the two poles are migrating, the Earth loses the magnetic shield that surrounds it, and that means we'll all be bombarded with cosmic rays and particles and we'll basically be sunburned to death.

Rhonda: And why is this on your list?

Alma: Well, it *has* been 780,000 years since the last reversal, so we're a bit overdue.

Rhonda: Dr Nassar, you're beginning to scare me! We have time for one more scenario.

Alma: Well, here's one I particularly like; it's not technically the Earth killing us off, but the laws of physics – but since the Earth certainly follows the laws of physics, I think it counts.

Rhonda: OK.

Alma: In a couple of places on Earth – on Long Island, about 100 kilometres east of New York City and in Switzerland near Geneva, for example – we have particle accelerators, where we test and stretch our knowledge of quantum physics. The problem is that we really don't have much experiential knowledge of quantum physics. Most of what we have is theoretical knowledge. But sometimes theories are wrong, and these particle accelerators might – just might – be able to generate enough energy to create a black hole that would devour the Earth. They might also be able to create a different type of matter – it's called 'strange matter' or 'strangelets' – that might, again might, just convert ordinary matter into strange matter on contact. There would be a runaway chain reaction in places where there is a lot of ordinary matter, like here on Earth. I doubt very much we'd be able to survive the conversion into strange matter.

Rhonda: So there we have three ways the Earth could wipe out humanity in the next 100 years. To learn about the other fascinating ways we could all become extinct, enrol for Dr Nassar's class ES312. Dr Alma Nassar, thank you for taking the time to talk with us. This is Rhonda Tyson and this has been the Faber College 'Know your faculty' podcast for the week of October 15th.

UNIT 5

The highlighted words in this unit's audio transcripts are words found in the Academic Word List.

Track 2.15

1 a phrase used to **reject** a proposition
2 **status** or reputation
3 be unsuccessful, as in baseball
4 something bad that happens

5 understanding
6 feeling of happiness or satisfaction
7 way of doing things
8 **final** result of a situation
9 unhappy that something is not better
10 develop or result in a certain way
11 the feeling that you are valuable

Track 2.16

Hi. My name's Bob, and I'm not an optimist. I think that I've always known that I'm not an optimist. And certainly my family has known for a long time! But it's taken me a long time to realize that not only do I not think that the glass is half full, I actually think that the glass will fall off the night stand, break, and in the morning when I wake up, I'm going to cut my feet on the broken glass.

I'm a pessimist. I'm also a lawyer, and the two are not unrelated. Some 20 years ago, William Eaton and his **colleagues** studied the connection between **occupation** and **depression**. Their **research** looked at 104 different **occupations** and found that the most **depressed** workers were lawyers, followed by special-ed teachers and secretaries.

Indeed, they found that lawyers suffered a **depression** rate 3.6 times higher than employed people generally. Not 3.6 *percent* higher, 3.6 *times*. To put it another way, for every 100 average workers that are **depressed**, there are 360 **depressed** lawyers.

Why? Well, the answer may just be the way we're trained. We're trained to be risk managers, to be risk limiters. Our clients come to us with a problem, and we sit down and we try to figure out what can go wrong, or go worse, and we try to find ways to avoid that **outcome**.

That training **apparently** starts even before we start practising law. Back in 1987, a study at the University of Virginia Law School found that pessimistic law students outperformed optimistic law students, even though optimists generally do better at university level.

The reason for that **achievement**, according to **psychologist** Dr Martin Seligman, might be that pessimists are more careful than optimists. And good lawyers, for the most part, are careful lawyers. Good lawyers plan on things going wrong.

But this pessimistic outlook has a downside. As Dr Seligman says in a report entitled 'Why Lawyers are Unhappy', 'the qualities that make for a good lawyer may not make for a happy human being'.

Now, Dr Seligman has been one of the most important figures in the development of **Positive Psychology**, and so he's spent a lot of his career studying happiness. And what he says is that when you spend all day at the office looking for the flaw, **anticipating** the worst-case **scenario**, it's very hard to turn that off when you leave.

What's more, when lawyers leave the office, they don't exactly enjoy good standing in the **community**. When people were polled about how honest different professions are, do you know what they said? They said nurses are honest. They said pharmacists are honest. What did they say about lawyers? They said that lawyers are less honest than auto mechanics. So lawyers do not have the same standing as nurses or even auto mechanics.

When we start with a tendency to look for what's wrong, and we add that low standing in the **community**, it can **create** a really vicious **cycle**. It's not hard to understand why lawyers might not think too highly of themselves. Low standing leads to low self-esteem. And given that low self-esteem, it's not hard to see why lawyers have a **depression** rate 3.6 times higher than the general population. Fortunately, it's not impossible to do something about this. The field of **Positive Psychology** has shown us how. Now, that doesn't mean it's easy to do something about this. It doesn't happen overnight. But Dr Seligman is **convinced** that we can learn to be more optimistic. To feel better. We can learn to turn off the pessimism when it's **inappropriate**, and turn it back on when it's to our advantage. This is important: Dr Seligman notes that pessimism carries advantages, too. Pessimists often have a more **accurate** view of reality than optimists, for example. This is a good thing to have on your side when your clients' future is at stake. Seligman also points out that pessimists are better at **evaluating** risks, which is, of course, a key **aspect** of being a successful lawyer.

So it's a question of finding a balance. Of finding a balance between optimism and pessimism. Of finding a good work–life balance, and using the time you spend with friends and family to get away from the negativity of the office.

The key to finding this balance is learning what Dr Seligman calls 'a disputing **technique**', which is **specifically designed** to counter your pessimistic ideas. As lawyers, we're quite familiar with disputes, and so this is a **technique** I think you can all get comfortable with. Let's move on now to how the disputing **technique** works.

Track 2.17

1 **Speaker 1:** Can I ask why no one in my department got a raise this year?

  Speaker 2: It's not because of your **job** performance, I can **assure** you. But owing to our losses in the Central Asian markets, the company just doesn't have the cash this year.

Track 2.18

2 André has only been a lawyer for two years. Still, he's the best litigator the firm has.

Track 2.19

3 **Speaker 1:** You know, Professor Hoyt, you give more homework than any other Criminology professor at this university.

  Speaker 2: On the other hand, I don't **require** you to attend court sessions.

Track 2.20

4 **Speaker 1:** Can you explain to me why there's a difference between the value of imports and **exports** on this **chart**? Shouldn't they be equal?

  Speaker 2: Not necessarily. **Exports** are calculated on their actual value, while tariffs are included in the calculation of imports.

Track 2.21

5 **Speaker 1:** I'm sorry, Professor, but I didn't really get what you were saying about the limits on **computer** size.

  Speaker 2: I see. Well, you're familiar with Moore's Law, aren't you?

  Speaker 1: The one that says that **computer** performance will double every 18 months, right?

  Speaker 2: Right. Now keep in mind that Moore's law

isn't a mathematical **constraint** – it refers more to the transistors used in **computers** – the storage space if you will – and their cost. The law of **diminishing** returns tells us that at a certain point, the cost of adding extra storage space will be higher than the added **benefit** of the additional space, and so there's going to come a time when **computer** performance doesn't double, because it won't be worth the cost of doubling it.

Track 2.22

6 **Speaker 1**: Three years ago, when we were negotiating our last **contract**, you promised us that the firm wouldn't cut health **benefits** for at least five years, yet here you are demanding a 15% reduction.

  Speaker 2: Be that as it may, the simple fact is that healthcare costs have gone up a lot in the last three years, and are promising to go up even more in the next few years. This company cannot remain competitive if we don't **adjust** the **benefits**.

Track 2.23

7 Over the past five years, we've seen a 37% increase in the number of applications to Faber College. The result is that we have seen the quality of Faber students increase **dramatically**. The SAT scores of incoming Faber students have risen from 1,065 five years ago to 1,225 today.

Track 2.24

8 There are close to 9,000 near-Earth objects that we know about so far. What's more, we know for a fact that asteroids have been responsible for nearly wiping out life on this planet in the past. Thus it's in everybody's best interest for the government to spend more money on asteroid-preparedness programmes.

Track 2.25

Good evening. For most of my **professional** life as a clinical **psychologist**, my **focus**, my profession's **focus**, was on helping people get better. That sounds like a worthy **goal**, and indeed it is. **Nevertheless**, it's a **goal** that often left me dissatisfied, for two reasons. The first is that it often seemed that too many of my patients didn't really get better. The understanding we have developed about chemistry and the brain has taught us that many of these patients needed better drug treatment, not a better therapist, which is fortunate for my self-esteem. The second reason for my dissatisfaction was an unanswered question: 'Why wasn't everybody in therapy?' Don't laugh. Back in those days, most **psychologists** believed that everybody needed therapy. But my experience had shown me that that wasn't true. There were people out there who didn't need me. And that realization led me to ask two additional questions: 'What did these people know, or do, that my patients didn't?' and 'Could my patients learn it?', whatever 'it' was. That 'it' is what I'd like to talk about tonight: learned optimism.

Track 2.26

… That 'it' is what I'd like to talk about tonight: learned optimism.
So, I'll start by saying that optimism is not about having a happy, smiley face. Let me repeat that: optimism is not about acting happy. I've got nothing against happy, smiley faces, but happy, smiley faces are an **outcome**, not a

strategy. People often confuse optimism with **positive** thinking, with the idea that if you act like it's true, then it will be true. You put on your happy face and repeat to yourself again and again 'My life is getting better each and every day', even if all the **evidence** is to the **contrary**. Maybe for some people that works, but I haven't met many of them. Most of the people I've met value **accuracy**. And there are going to be times in our lives when today is decidedly not better than yesterday.
So that's what optimism isn't. Turning to what it is, let me say that optimism is simply a **strategy** to explain to ourselves what happens in our world: the things that have gone right and – especially – the things that have gone wrong. It turns out that if we can look at the adversity in our life, see it as **temporary** rather than permanent, see it as something that **affects** only a **portion** of our lives and not our entire being, and see it as something that we can do something about, then we will live happier lives. Remember these three things, they're important: adversity is **temporary**, it doesn't affect every **aspect** of our life, and it's something we can do something about. We'll come back to explore them in a little while.
So, so much for what optimism is. Now let's move on to my second question all those years ago: 'Can optimism be learned?' Well, since we're talking about a **strategy** called 'learned optimism', I guess the answer is obvious. Yes, you can learn how to apply an optimistic **strategy** to the events in your life, and it turns out that learning how doesn't **require** much more than a notebook, some attention and some patience. What **research** has shown is that optimists and pessimists differ in their explanations in three key **areas**, which I like to call the 'three Ps'.

Track 2.27

… What **research** has shown is that optimists and pessimists differ in their explanations in three key **areas**, which I like to call the 'three Ps'.
The first P is permanence. When optimists are faced with some adversity, they see that adversity as something **temporary**, and not something that will be in their lives forever. Pessimists, on the other hand, tend to think that the adversity will always be there.
The second 'P' is what we call pervasiveness. When a pessimist strikes out with a girl, he tells himself 'I'm unattractive'; when an optimist strikes out with the same girl, he says 'I'm not attractive to *her*.'
In other words, the pessimist treats that moment of adversity as a general problem, something to be **found** in all **aspects** of his life. For the optimist, though, the adversity is not a pervasive problem in his life, it's **unique** to that situation, to that girl.
Finally, there's personalization, the third 'P'. Pessimists tend to blame themselves when bad things happen; optimists, on the other hand, are apt to blame someone else, not themselves. Personalization is what happens when you go round thinking that it's all your fault.
Now, before we move on to tackling the problems of the three 'Ps', let's recap what we've seen so far …

Track 2.28

Mandy: What makes you happy seems to be a very personal question. After all, we all have different tastes; different things give us pleasure. I like watching the sun rise all by myself; you prefer a late evening in a disco with all your friends. And yet, when scientists began to look at the question of happiness scientifically, **research** showed that while there may not be many absolute keys to happiness, there are, indeed, common key **factors** that lead to happiness. Our guests today, Drs Ye-Jun Park and Martina Diaz, both from the Faber College **Psychology** Department, have been studying happiness for the past nine years, and have raised an interesting question in their studies, namely, 'Why aren't we happier?'. Dr Park, Dr Diaz, welcome.

Dr Diaz: Thank you, Mandy.

Mandy: How did you get started on your **research**?

Dr Park: Well, originally, it came out of a shared love for Tolstoy. You see, Tolstoy famously observed that unhappy families are each unhappy in their own way. Martina and I, as **psychologists** and Tolstoy fans, both knew the **quote**, and wondered if it was really true. Is unhappiness **unique**?

Mandy: Is it?

Dr Diaz: Well, Tolstoy had much more **insight** into the human condition that I will ever have, so I have no desire to **contradict** him. **Nevertheless**, it turns out that there are a number of common mistakes we make that make our worlds less happy than they could be.

Mandy: In fact, in your **research**, you list four key reasons why humans are bad at answering the question 'What will make me happy?'.

Dr Diaz: That's right, Mandy. The first reason is that we're not particularly good at calculating probability. For example, let me ask you a question: are you more likely to win the lottery or die from a meteor hitting your house?

Mandy: Well, neither is very likely, and I know that scientists love **statistics** like this, so I'll say 'get hit by a meteor'.

Dr Park: I'm afraid not; you're more likely to win the lottery. The **odds** are really small – one in 13,983,816 – but they're still better than the **odds** of a meteor hitting your house, which have been **estimated** at more than 182 trillion to one. But how about a more everyday **scenario**: are you more likely to die in the next year because of an accident **involving transportation** or because of any other type of accident?

Mandy: I have no idea. You certainly hear about **transportation** accidents a lot.

Dr Park: Yes, you do. But the chances you'll die in a transport-related accident in the next year are 77 to one. Non-transport-related? Sixty-nine to one. So you're more likely to die in a non-transport related accident. And we still have another question: are 77 to one and 69 to one good **odds** or **odds** that we should be worried about?

Mandy: How does calculating probability **affect** our happiness?

Dr Diaz: Well, the **odds** are important if we want to determine which things we should be doing in order to increase our happiness. We should be **focusing** our efforts on doing things that have a good probability of being successful. Because **research** shows that we're happier when we actually **achieve** our **goals**. But because our brains aren't really **designed** for calculating **odds**, we often spend a lot of time and effort trying to **achieve** things that we probably won't **achieve**. In addition, we

spend a lot of time and effort worrying about things that are remote possibilities, like worrying about getting eaten by a shark at the beach, rather than **focusing** on the adverse events that are much more likely, like getting sunburned at the beach.

Mandy: So we'd be happier if we studied **statistics**?

Dr Park: Let's just say that our instinctive **approach** when it comes to **statistics** is an obstacle to our happiness.

Dr Diaz: It turns out that we're also not very good at **estimating** value. And this is obstacle number two to our happiness.

Mandy: What do you mean?

Dr Diaz: Mm. Let's say you're walking down the street, and you pass an art gallery, and you see a small painting that you like. You walk in and ask how much it costs. And the lady in the gallery tells you that it **normally** costs 1,500 euros, but because they have to renovate the gallery for a new **exhibit**, it's on sale for 1,200 euros. So you buy the painting because that's a pretty good deal.
Now imagine an **alternative scenario**. Same gallery, same painting, same starting price: 1,500 euros. But because the gallery owner has had a big argument with the artist, the gallery is willing to sell the painting for 750 euros. You go away and think about the painting, and decide that it'll look very good over the **computer** in your office and so you go back to the gallery the next day to buy the painting. And the nice lady there informs you that the gallery owner and the artist have settled their differences, and that the painting now costs 1,100 euros. Would you still buy it?

Mandy: No, probably not.

Dr Park: You and most other people. There's no way that you will spend 1,100 euros today for something you could have had for 750 euros yesterday. And yet 1,100 euros is a better deal than the deal you accepted: 1,200 euros. We base our ideas of value on what happened yesterday, not what something is worth today.

Mandy: How should we calculate value?

Dr Park: Value depends on what else you can do with that money at that moment, not what you could have done with the money at another time in the past.

Mandy: We're talking with Drs Ye-Jun Park and Martina Diaz from Faber College about why we aren't as happy as we could be. When we come back, we'll talk about two more common mistakes we make about our happiness. And we'll also be taking your calls. So please don't go anywhere. We'll be back in two minutes.

UNIT 6

Track 3.1

1 advertisement
2 campaign
3 consumers
4 image
5 launch
6 competitive advantage
7 motto
8 product
9 promotion
10 rebranding
11 sales
12 life cycle

Track 3.2

Speaker 1: How does rebranding work, then?

Speaker 2: Well, let me start by giving you a couple of examples. First, let's talk about rats.

Speaker 1: Rats?

Speaker 2: Yes, the common rat. Not too long ago, there was an ad campaign that was targeted at improving the image of the common rat.

Speaker 1: You're kidding!

Speaker 2: No, it was a serious campaign. Well, it was run as a serious campaign. There was a website – www.greatpointedarcher.com – there were videos, there was even a full-page ad in *Advertising Age*.

Speaker 1: What was that website?

Speaker 2: www.greatpointedarcher.com. 'Great pointed archer' is all one word, by the way.

Speaker 1: Why, what was the point?

Speaker 2: Well, according to the website, the aim was to increase the empathy people feel for – and I quote – the much-maligned rat. In fact, they ran a print ad that had a drawing of a little girl cuddling a puppy. She has a hot drink and some biscuits, and outside it's a dark, rainy night. And pressed against the window pane, staring in, is a rat. And the caption reads: 'Everyone wants to be warm and dry'.

Speaker 1: No way!

Speaker 2: Oh yes. And wait, there's more. The website offered merchandise, including T-shirts, thongs, mouse pads and cookies.

Speaker 1: Why was the website named 'greatpointedarcher.com'?

Speaker 2: Because that's the name they want to change 'rats' to. You see, according to the campaign, one of the problems that rats have is that the word 'rat' itself isn't very noble. And so, if the name of the animal were changed to 'great pointed archer', well then, people would feel differently about the animal.

Speaker 1: Is this really a legitimate campaign?

Speaker 2: That's an excellent question. The campaign dates back to 2005, and quite a few people in the advertising world are convinced that it was a hoax designed to highlight some ad agency. But no one ever admitted to it, and they went to great lengths to make it seem legitimate, even getting an expert on rats involved, not to mention PETA, People for the Ethical Treatment of Animals. There was a 30-second video spot that showed a party – with rats – and when the rats find humans eating their food, they all run out of the apartment. A lot of thought went into this.

Speaker 1: How strange! Well, we were talking before we went on air about how the European Union decided to rebrand. Can you tell us something about that?

Speaker 2: Of course. Well, for this one, you have to go back to 1998. The European Union had been the European Union for just a few years (before 1993, the EU was the EC) and it had a flag, and it had *Ode to Joy*, that classic Beethoven piece, as its anthem. But the flag and the anthem had been used by the EC, so it was decided that a motto was needed, a symbol that was connected only to this new European institution. And so, well, they ran a contest for schoolchildren, for them to come up with the motto, and at the end of the contest 'Unity in diversity' was the winner. It was even included in the constitution.

Speaker 1: So what do rats and the European Union have in common?

Speaker 2: I think they both point to the fundamental question: Why rebrand? In the EU's case, it seems that people in Brussels thought that a new generation of Europeans needed a new justification for the European Union, that the older sales pitch of preventing any more World War IIs just didn't resonate any more. Rebranding is a powerful way of breaking with the past. As Lew Platt once said, 'Whatever made you successful in the past, won't in the future.' So one reason to choose rebranding is to stay relevant and keep up with changing consumer needs. That's what Lew Platt was talking about. Another reason, and we see this with the EU, is the perception that a brand has become old-fashioned.

Speaker 1: And as for the rats?

Speaker 2: Well, of course, another reason to break with the past is because the past has negative connotations for your brand.

Speaker 1: What are some of the other reasons organizations have for rebranding?

Speaker 2: Mergers and acquisitions is one: takeovers, including cases where one of the brands basically disappears and the other brand has to take on that identity as well.

Speaker 1: Does globalization play a role?

Speaker 2: It certainly does. A classic example is the Marathon bar. Now, Marathon was one of Great Britain's most popular chocolate bars, but in the US, they were sold as Snickers. So here, on the one hand, you had Marathon, with a long tradition in the UK; on the other hand, you had Snickers, which happened to be the world's biggest-selling candy bar. Two brands, one bar. And eventually, M&M/Mars took the decision to rebrand Marathon as Snickers.
Another reason to rebrand is because the organization wants to signal that it's going in a new direction. Phillip Morris decides that it doesn't want to be a tobacco company any more, and all of a sudden Altria is trading on the New York Stock Exchange.

Speaker 1: Does rebranding work?

Speaker 2: I think that really depends. There are so many different ways to rebrand – from changing your logo or your packaging all the way to changing the company name and what products and services you offer – that it's really hard to give a blanket answer. I think it really depends on your reasons for rebranding.
With every rebranding effort, it's important to remember that there's already a brand – there's already something, in other words, which has some value, and if you're not careful, you run the risk of destroying the value of the old brand without generating increased value with the new.

Speaker 1: Will we be calling our local great-pointed-archer exterminator in the future?

Speaker 2: I doubt it. Not any time soon.

Speaker 1: Thank you, Dr Wilkinson, for stopping by today.

Track 3.3

1 Speaker 1: Can you tell me how long it takes to get a Bachelor of Science degree in the US?

Speaker 2: Well, in general, Bachelor's degrees are four-year degrees, but in the US, universities have quite a bit of latitude in deciding what their requirements for a degree are, so some Bachelor programmes can take longer.

2 Astronomers originally calculated an impact probability of 2.7%; that is, there was a one-in-37 chance that the asteroid would hit the Earth.

Track 3.5

3 … if you look hard enough, you'll see that artists have always liked to put extra information in their work. As we've already seen, Easter eggs are fairly common in computer software and on DVDs, but did you know that Alfred Hitchcock gave himself a cameo in almost 40 of the films he directed, or that Michelangelo included a cross-section of the human brain in his famous God-creating-Adam scene?

Track 3.6

4 Even in the US, with its First Amendment, the right of Free Speech is not as absolute as some people would like you to believe. There is, for instance, the famous example of not being able to yell 'fire' in a crowded theatre.

Track 3.7

5 **Speaker 1:** Did you understand why market share is so important?

Speaker 2: I think so. It goes without saying that the higher your market share, the more of your product you sell. But on top of that – and this is really the key – it turns out that the higher your market share, the higher your profitability.

Track 3.8

1 Since many words and phrases have more than one meaning, it can be difficult for the audience to determine which meaning the speaker wants to convey, especially when they are second-language users.

Track 3.9

2 The word 'motto' comes from Italian, and it was originally a pledge. To put it another way, your motto, or your group's motto, was a formal statement of what it wanted to be or to accomplish.

Track 3.10

3 **Speaker 1:** So, what did you think of the way the students performed in the test?

Speaker 2: Well, of course, I was shocked that Peter failed, but I was just as shocked that Petra passed. It was almost like they'd exchanged their test papers.

Track 3.11

4 **Speaker 1:** You seem to know quite a bit about making pizza.

Speaker 2: Well, pizza and I go way back together. In fact, I spent most of my teenage years working in my Uncle Sal's pizzeria after school.

Track 3.12

5 The most important software on your computer is the operating system – programs such as OSX, Windows and Linux, which allow you to interact with all the other programs on the computer.

Track 3.13

6 **Speaker 1:** So your students don't have to do their homework.

Speaker 2: That's right. Or rather, homework isn't included in the calculation of the final grade. I'd like to think that the homework is integral to the understanding of the course material, though.

Track 3.14

7 The use of subliminal advertising has been debated for decades. The main thing to remember about subliminal advertising is that so far, no one has proved that subliminal messages can get you to do something that you don't want to do.

Track 3.15

Before we get into the question of how to rebrand your products, I think it's worth taking a few minutes to explore the question of why we have brands in the first place. Brands are basically the way that companies have of identifying their products in the marketplace. The word 'brand' has become a bit of a dirty word in recent years, in part because of the success a few years back of *No Logo*. Do any of you remember the book? It was published in 2000 – wow, that sounds like such a long time ago, doesn't it? – and it focused on the connections between brands and globalization. Or rather, I should say that it focused on the negative influence of big brands, and tied a number of the bad things that big brands do to globalization.

But *No Logo* wasn't the first book to take brands to task. Anti-brand books, such as the classic *The Hidden Persuaders*, have been around since the 1950s. *The Hidden Persuaders* is the book that introduced a lot of people to the concept of subliminal advertising, which, if you'd like a working definition, would be the inclusion in an advertisement of any sensory stimuli not designed to be perceived consciously. To put it another way, subliminal advertising is adding words or images that are targeted at your subconscious, and not your conscious. For years after *The Hidden Persuaders* came out, people went through advertisements with a fine-tooth comb, trying to spot the subliminal messages. Subliminal advertising had that element of manipulation, and the result was a lot of bad press for marketing, and for brands.

But anyway, let's get back to the question of why we have brands. Historically, the concept of a brand as we mean it – which, as I mentioned before, is the concept of an identification for your particular product in the mass market – that concept of brand goes back to the mid-1800s. So, what happened in the mid-1800s to make brands worthwhile? Well, about that time, distribution networks greatly expanded, as a result of steam ships and railroads, and, broadly speaking, the spread of industrialization broke the one-on-one relationships that consumers had had with producers and with merchants.

Track 3.16

Well, about that time, distribution networks greatly expanded, as a result of steam ships and railroads, and, broadly speaking, the spread of industrialization broke the one-on-one relationships that consumers had had with producers and with merchants.

For example, factory-produced goods meant that the artisan that you knew was good no longer produced an item especially for you. And, especially in the big cities of

America and the UK, bigger department stores meant that there was no more 'shop owner' who knew your tastes and requirements. What's more, without that shop-owner point of reference, there was no one particular person that you knew was responsible for choosing the goods for sale. In that context, brands became a guarantee of quality and – more importantly – of consistency. You knew that a can of Shaker's-brand soup, for instance, that you bought in March would have the same quality and the same taste as the one you had bought in January. And in the absence of other relationships, the brand was the one thing you could rely on to make sure that your money was well spent. To put it another way, brands were a consumer-protection policy.

So why has something that was originally a benefit for the consumer developed such negative connotations? Well, one reason is competition. When Shaker's started off, for instance, its only real competition was home-made or restaurant-made soup. Do you know how many brands of canned soup there are today? Neither do I. There are too many to even begin counting.

And that means that consumers are just being bombarded today with information about brands. It's been estimated that every day, we all see or hear 1,500 advertisements, or better, marketing promotions. How is your brand going to be noticed in that brand-name soup?

The other big reason is quality control. As I mentioned before, the biggest advantage that brands offered customers was the guarantee of consistency. But over time, quality control spread throughout the industry. In other words, Shaker's soups offered you a certain quality and a certain consistency, but, as the production of canned soup became standardized, so did Bohnen soups and My Tie soups and literally hundreds of other canned-soup brands on the market today. The consistency that Shaker's promised way back when wasn't so special any more.

So your big competitive advantage isn't so advantageous any more, and you have a lot more competitors competing against you. This is a big problem. After all, the whole idea of a brand is to differentiate your product from the competition, but right now, you're not looking all that different. Fortunately for brand managers everywhere, after World War II, researchers began looking at the relationship that consumers developed with the brands they used, and began to explore concepts like brand image and brand loyalty.

And so you had the marketing departments taking over, and companies started focusing on building brands, not making products. And in fact, one of the biggest problems that big brands face today is that sense that they've outsourced everything. Bowl-a-Soup sure spends a lot on advertising its microwave-safe soup bowls, for instance, but who makes those soup bowls? Is it Bowl-a-Soup itself, or are they really made in some factory in China?

So, to sum up, three big problems for brands these days: a lot of competition; not always a lot of difference in the products; and a sense out there that you aren't really making your product anyway. And yet the motivation for brands remains. The motivation remains because people still want to know that their money is being well spent. Now, before we move on to the questions of why and how you should rebrand, let's look at what spending their money well means for your customers.

CONSOLIDATION 2

Track 3.17

Naomi: Excuse me, Professor Aoun, can I bother you for a few moments?

Professor Aoun: Of course, how can I help you?

Naomi: I'm a student in your Introduction to Linguistics class. It's about your lecture on universal grammar last week. I've listened to it a few times, but I still don't think I get it.

Professor Aoun: OK, well, let's see what you can tell me about it, and we can take it from there.

Naomi: Well, that's just the thing. I'm not even sure of what I know and what I don't.

Professor Aoun: Er, well, um, I'm sorry, what was your name?

Naomi: Naomi, Naomi Skinner.

Professor Aoun: Well, Naomi, let's start at the beginning. When we talk about language universals, what are we talking about?

Naomi: We're talking about language elements that you can find in every language, right?

Professor Aoun: I think it's better to think of them as the basic design features we can find in all languages.

Naomi: And this is where I start to get confused. What's the difference?

Professor Aoun: The difference is that when we talk about elements, we tend to think about the surface structure of the language – how the language uses tenses, for example, or whether it has gender or another classification system, how it identifies the roles in a sentence, and so on. And at the surface there are just so many different things we can do with language that it would be impossible, or almost impossible, to find an element that is universal to all languages.

Naomi: So universal grammar doesn't mean that every language has the same grammar?

Professor Aoun: No, of course not. But here, you have to be careful. 'Grammar' doesn't mean the same thing to a linguist that it normally does to a language student.

Naomi: It doesn't?

Professor Aoun: No. When linguists use the term 'grammar', we usually mean it in very broad terms, not just whether *fork* is a masculine noun or a feminine noun. In linguistics, the grammar is the system that the speakers use to produce the language.

Naomi: OK, I think I understand the difference. But aren't you saying that all languages are different?

Professor Aoun: Of course. But now the question becomes: 'Despite their differences, what, if anything, do languages have in common?' So, for example, we look at all the different ways that languages have for structuring their sentences – how some, like English, put the subject first in the sentence, then the verb, and then the object. This is an S-V-O language. But other languages, like Japanese, are S-O-V: they put the object before the verb. And you can have other languages that put the verb in the first position, V-S-O. Modern Irish does that, for instance. And you can look at these differences, and not even notice that you've identified four very important universals.

Naomi: I'm lost.

Professor Aoun: Well, think about it. We're comparing the different ways that languages structure their subjects, verbs and objects. That means we can say that, syntactically, all languages have a structure that we can compare, and that in every language we can find something that functions as a subject, functions as a verb, functions as an object.

So, in syntax, we see that there are universals. We move to pronunciation, and we see that every language has vowels, every language has consonants, every language has syllables, every language has stress. And we can move to other aspects and we can find other universals. For example, vocabulary: did you know that all languages have pronouns?

Naomi: Forgive me, but these universals seem rather simplistic.

Professor Aoun: Well, they would, wouldn't they? But these are what is known as absolute universals. They're true for every language. More interesting are the universals that we call 'implicational universals'.

Naomi: Implicational universals?

Professor Aoun: Yes. Now, I know that 'implicational universal' has a scary sound, but it's not really as abstract as the term implies. Let me give you an example. Not every language has affixes – elements that are added to a base word, like when we take the verb *teach* and we add *–er* to make *teacher*.

Naomi: I understand.

Professor Aoun: Now, there are a lot of different affixes. You can have suffixes like *–er*, prefixes like *un–*, and there are other affixes used in other languages that we don't use in English. Some languages have inflexes, for example, where you put the element inside the base word. So, not every language uses affixes, and not every language uses every type of affix.

Naomi: OK …

Professor Aoun: But here's something interesting. Some languages only use suffixes. And all the languages that only use suffixes are postpositional languages.

Naomi: Postpositional?

Professor Aoun: Hmm. In English we use prepositions, don't we? We say *to Cambridge*. We put the preposition first and the noun second. But other languages are post-positional: they say *Cambridge to*. In other words, they put the noun first and their preposition, or 'postposition', second.

Naomi: OK, I understand.

Professor Aoun: So we have a sort of condition: if a language uses only suffixes, then that language will be postpositional, not prepositional. And that's what we mean by implicational universal – if a language has one element, then it will have another.

Naomi: So language universals are basically patterns that we find in languages, aren't they? Sometimes every language has a certain pattern, and sometimes if a language has one pattern, then it will have another. Have I got this right?

Professor Aoun: Yes, I think you do. Now, one caveat. Not everyone agrees that there are language universals. Their basic criticism is that we haven't fully studied every language, so we're not really in a position to claim that there are language universals. And they do have a point. After all, if we can find even one exception to a certain universal, then it isn't so universal, is it?

Naomi: What do you think, Professor Aoun?

Professor Aoun: I think that we all have the same brains, Naomi. And we all learn our mother tongue in more or less the same way. So it makes sense to me that there are commonalities. However, we can talk about that some more at the lecture next week. Now, is there anything else you need help with?

Naomi: No, that's fine, Professor. Thank you very much for your time.

Track 3.18

1 also
2 so
3 in other words
4 It goes without saying that …
5 after all
6 even if
7 but
8 indeed
9 On the other hand, …
10 and
11 such as
12 As I mentioned before, …

Track 3.19

Why do languages die? The simplistic answer is that a language dies because it has no more native speakers. The reason this answer is simplistic is because it doesn't offer an explanation as to *why* people have stopped speaking the language.

The process of language death is usually a gradual one. A community becomes bilingual and, over time, switches from its original language to the new one. Eventually, the people of the community stop using their native tongue altogether. This assimilation, as it's called, can bring about the death of the native language.

Why does the community assimilate the new language? Economic and social reasons are high on the list. People, particularly adults, communicate to a large degree in order to conduct business and to socialize. Once a new language becomes the language of business and social contact, the older language can quickly find itself in danger.

Is an endangered language a dying language? Not necessarily. There have been efforts to revitalize a number of languages, including Hebrew, Welsh and even Navajo. How successful these efforts have been is open to debate, but it's clear that a dying language strikes a chord and makes us reflect on what language means to us.

Track 3.20

I grew up speaking Vietnamese. Most of you grew up speaking English. And one of the great questions of linguistics is whether our respective languages determine the way we see the world.

This question is known in academic circles as the question of 'linguistic determinism'. It's a question that goes back centuries, and I think that it's a question that goes to the heart of what makes us human.

So let's look at this important question and see if we can find some answers. And let's start by asking ourselves what this linguistic determinism would look like. At its most basic, linguistic determinism says that our language tells us what we can – and cannot – talk about.

In the 1940s, it seemed as though linguists had found a scientific basis to support the concept of linguistic determinism. An American linguist – Benjamin Lee Whorf – published a paper in which he said that work he'd done with Edward Sapir proved that the concept that Native Americans have of reality is very different from the concept English speakers have of reality – speakers of most western European languages, actually.

This was a very powerful claim. In fact, it was so powerful that linguistic determinism soon became known as the Sapir-Whorf hypothesis. Whorf explained that the structure of Native American languages left their speakers unable to understand the concept of time that was so absolutely essential to English speakers. Let me stress that. He was not saying that they were lacking a particular word that we have in English. He was saying that Hopis could not understand time the way we understand time in English.

The Hopi language, according to Whorf, didn't have any grammatical reference to past, present or future. It didn't even have *words* for past, present or future, and that meant that the Hopis were unable to conceive of the flow of time the same way English speakers could.

Whorf, by the way, was also responsible for the popularity of the Eskimo snow story. Do you know this story, about how the Eskimos – or Inuits, as I guess we should call them – have 27 words for snow, or 200, or even 400? The point was that Inuits have many more words for snow than we do, and thus see snow differently than we do.

But there were some problems with the Sapir-Whorf hypothesis. Apparently, Whorf was much more enthusiastic than he was meticulous. It turns out, for example, that he only spoke with one Hopi speaker, and that was a neighbour of his in New York City. Turns out, too, that Inuit doesn't have any more words for snow than English does and that Inuits see snow the same way English speakers do.

So was linguistic determinism wrong? Well, let me repeat what Whorf was saying. He was saying that the language we speak determines the way we see the world, the way we 'dissect nature', to borrow his words. In other words, Inuits do not see snow differently than you and I do because they live with the stuff 365 days a year, and we live with it for a few snowy weekends in February. They see snow differently than we do precisely because they have more words for it than we do, and those additional words force them to see it differently. What's more, because we don't have those additional words in English, we have no ability to comprehend those different ways.

Now, let's look at an alternative. Language serves a number of different functions, but its primary function is probably information management. There's a lot of information out there in reality, and no finite language system can address all of it at any one time. There's information about the timing of an event. There's information about whether that event is a regular event or a one-off. There's information about the people in the event and the things. There's information about the spatial relationships between those people and those things. There's information about motion, about causation, about the relationship between the people having the conversation – how well they know each other, for example. There's even information about how we know the information itself – did we see the event, take part in it, hear about it from our Hopi neighbour in New York, or what?

So languages pay attention to a selection of the information available, not to all the information available. In the words of another important linguist, Roman Jakobson, 'Languages differ essentially in what they must convey.' To put it another way, when I produce a sentence in English, I must put at least one verb in some form of the past, present or future. If I don't, then I don't have a grammatical sentence. The grammar of English says I must give you information about time. And that means that I have to pay attention to time when I produce a sentence in English. Hopi speakers don't.

On the other hand, I don't have to worry about whether I need to address you as *vous* or *tu*, like I would in French. I can just use *you*. The grammar of French requires me to pay attention to how well I know you. The grammar of English doesn't.

This is the weak version of linguistic determinism. It's the idea that our language gets us to pay attention to certain aspects of reality, and that what we're paying attention to colours our reality in some way. This version has been tested and seems to be true. In one experiment, psychologists asked speakers of German, French and Spanish to associate voices and characteristics with some inanimate nouns, like bridges, forks and rain. Why German, French and Spanish? Well, they all use masculine and feminine gender to mark their nouns. I hope I don't have to point out to you that grammatical gender doesn't necessarily refer to boys and girls, but in this case, sex does play a role, because it turns out that the nouns in the experiment had contrasting genders in two of the languages. That means that if *bridge* is feminine in German and *fork* is feminine in French – which they are – then they will be masculine in Spanish, which they are.

What do you think the experimenters found? They found that Spanish speakers tended to attribute more 'manly' characteristics to masculine nouns like *bridge* (strength was one), while Germans tended to go with more 'female' characteristics, like elegance. And masculine Spanish forks speak with deeper voices than feminine French forks.

This does not mean, of course, that German speakers think that their bridges are girls. But it does suggest that German speakers might make associations about inanimate objects that would never occur to speakers of non-gender languages like English. Of course – and this is very important – we need to keep in mind that once the association is pointed out to the speaker of another language, that speaker is perfectly capable of understanding the association. After all, you all just understood what I was saying about German bridges, right? We're paying attention to different aspects of the same reality.

I'd like to move on to some other areas where this weak linguistic determinism might work, but before I move on, does anybody have any questions?

Answer key

UNIT 1

Vocabulary focus
1 1 major 2 tuition 3 enrol 4 graduate 5 degree
2 a Excerpt 2 b Excerpt 6 c Excerpt 4 d Excerpt 8
e Excerpt 1 f Excerpt 3 g Excerpt 5 h Excerpt 7
3 1 e 2 h 3 a 4 d 5 c 6 f 7 g

Going further
Suggested answer: grade point average = average of the grades received for all the courses taken (often based on a four-point system)

Practise your listening
1 1 b 2 c 3 a 4 c 5 a 6 b 7 a
2 1 (roughly) 1,600 2 (about) 8,000 3 1948
4 application(s) 5 financial aid 6 Statistics
7 Behavioural Economics 8 Biochemistry
3 *Suggested answers*
1 **Engineering:** Calculus; Dynamics of Machines; Management of Technology
2 **Business Management:** Ethics; Organizational Staffing; Principles of Accounting
3 **Media Arts:** Directing for the Screen; History of the Documentary; Themes in Literature and Film
4 **Psychology:** Biological Sciences; The Science of the Mind; Research Methods

Language focus
1 See audio transcript for Track 10 (page 86).

Going further
One hundred and twenty-three trillion, one hundred and twenty-three billion, one hundred and twenty-three million, one hundred and twenty-three thousand, one hundred and twenty-three
3 1 b 2 b 3 a 4 a 5 a 6 b
5 *Suggested answers*
1 just over 9,100; approximately 9,000
2 nearly 30,000; close to 30,000
3 roughly 43 billion; over 42.8 billion
4 around 307,000; more than 300,000

Going further
Suggested answers
Student A
1 nearly 360,000
2 close to 100 million dollars
3 just over 3,000
4 almost 8 billion dollars
5 –
6 approximately 9.5 trillion kilometres
Student B
1 over 285,000
2 –
3 just over three
4 more than 22.5 million dollars
5 just over 5,400 euros
6 almost 5.9 trillion miles
The numbers that can't be rounded off are 4,500 (Student A) and 2,700 (Student B). They both end in 00 so are 'rounded off' already.

Listening for production
1 1 a year 2 a type of degree 3 a number 4 a number
5 a field of study 6 a number 7 a field of study
8 an amount of money (in dollars)

2 1 1636 2 Bachelor of Arts 3 1,524,092 4 2,675
5 Business 6 close to / c. 164,000 7 Library Science
8 $13,424
3 a 5 b 1 c 7 d 3 e 8 f 6 g 2 h 4

Listening for meaning
1 a 9 b 4 c 7 d 6 e 2 f 5 g 8 h 10 i 3 j 1
2 1 founded 2 not to mention 3 has been around
4 number-one 5 care about 6 requires (something)
3 1 b 2 a 3 b 4 b 5 a

Unit extension
2 1 (a) balance sheet 2 asset(s) 3 Marketing
4 should be selling / should sell 5 (a) big-picture
6 your money should be 7 Finance 8 loses value
9 express yourself / your ideas 10 in the door
3 *Sample answers*
1 One of the keys to earning money is understanding what you have, and what you need financially. Accounting teaches you to understand the difference between an asset and a liability, and how to read a balance sheet, so that you have a clear idea of what your financial situation is.
2 Economics courses give you an idea of the big picture, of where the economy is, and how it got there. This information is important for figuring out which investments you should put your money in.
3 Good writing gets you in the door. In business, a lot of communication is done through writing. Expressing yourself clearly – and correctly – is essential if you want people to listen to you, and perhaps buy what you have to sell.
5 1 b 2 c 3 c 4 a 5 b 6 b

Going further
1 conception, concepts, conceptual, conceptualization, conceptualize, conceptualized, conceptualizes, conceptualizing, conceptually
2 invested, investing, investment, investments, investor, investors, invests, reinvest, reinvested, reinvesting, reinvestment, reinvests
3 consume, consumed, consumer, consumers, consumes, consuming

UNIT 2

Vocabulary focus
1 1 e 2 f 3 b 4 a 5 – 6 d 7 c

Going further
Suggested definition for *show* = live performance
2 1 book 2 cover 3 go 4 sell out 5 have
4 1 c 2 d 3 f 4 a 5 b 6 e

Practise your listening
1 1 c 2 b 3 b 4 a 5 a
2 1 in San Diego, on March 28th 2 three 3 55,347
4 close to $6 million / nearly $6 million / etc.

Language focus
1 A
2 1 Talk to / Contact people 4 Do research
3 2 local promoters 3 universities
5 organized/reliable system 6 where and when?
7 out-of-town bands

Listening for production

1 1 b 2 c 3 c 4 a

2 1 Where did Short Shrift start the tour (before moving east to Ontario)?
2 Overall, how many shows did the band play in Canada?
3 Why did the band start the tour in Canada?
4 How long had it been since the band was on tour?
5 Whose comeback tour did the band spend some time opening for?
6 Which show was the only sell-out?
7 How much did the tour gross?
8 How will the band make a profit?

3 1 British Columbia / western Canada
2 29
3 they weren't able to get American visas in time
4 over four years
5 the Funky Knights / the Funky Nights
6 Montreal
7 around 1.2 million Canadian dollars
8 selling the music from the shows online

5 1 Promoting a particular show
2 Any two from: Venue / Equipment / Security
3 Fine Arts
4 Business Law / Decisions in History
5 Almost 12 years
6 Opening acts
7 80–20 / 70–30

Going further

Sample answer

A 'door split' is one way for bands and promoters to be paid. In a door split, the band and the promoter each get a percentage of ticket sales. Generally, the band gets a bigger percentage, but expenses also need to be considered. Sometimes the expenses will be deducted before the ticket sales are split. Other times, the expenses are taken out of the promoter's percentage.

Listening for meaning

1 1 job descriptions 2 not quite sure
3 good working relationships 4 put on a show
5 in order 6 one thing led to another
7 take [two] courses; a big help 8 laid the foundation
9 main thing; fine print 10 go through the contract

3 1 in order 2 good working relationship 3 fine print
4 job description 5 one thing leads to another
6 lay the foundation 7 big help

4 1 crunching 2 bask (in) 3 (very) good 4 grand
5 held 6 not bad

Unit extension

1 4

2 A 1 B 2 C 3

3 1 55 2 Max Yasgur 3 Roberts 4 Lang 5 10,000
6 186,000 7 got/received refunds 8 31,240 9 5.07 p.m.
10 Iron Butterfly 11 400,000–500,000 12 600

4 1 600 acres 2 *New York Times* and *Wall Street Journal*
3 Build a recording studio 4 $500,000
5 Thursday August 14th (the night before the festival was scheduled to begin) 6 three

5 1 Bethel, NY 2 Friday August 15th / 15th August
3 Sunday August 17th / 17th August 4 Jimi Hendrix
5 Roberts 6 *New York Times* / *Wall Street Journal*
7 *Wall Street Journal* / *New York Times*
8 recording studio 9 30 10 Iron Butterfly 11 400,000
12 500,000 13 people died 14 186,000 15 2.6 million

Going further

2 Sweetwater 3 Canned Heat 4 Mountain
5 The Grateful Dead 6 10 Years After
7 The Grease Band 8 Sly and the Family Stone
9 Jefferson Airplane 10 Blood, Sweat and Tears
11 The Who

UNIT 3

Topic focus

3 a civil law b common law c religious law

Vocabulary focus

1 1 b 2 a 3 a 4 b 5 c 6 a 7 c 8 b

2 Lawyer 1: environmental Lawyer 2: labour
Lawyer 3: criminal Lawyer 4: maritime
Lawyer 5: business

Practise your listening

1 1 e 2 c 3 f 4 a 5 b

2 1 be a good citizen 2 proposal 3 get/be involved
4 Report Stage 5 Royal Assent
6 witheld assent / refused to make the Bill an Act

Language focus

1 B

2 1 legislation 2 written 3 judges' decisions 4 Roman
5 6th century 6 force of law

Going further

Sample answer

The smallest state in Europe is not Liechtenstein, Andorra or San Marino. It's not even the Vatican City. The smallest state in Europe is an old British sea fort from World War II, located in the North Sea about 10 kilometres off the coast of England.

The Principality of Sealand began life in 1967, when Roy Bates took over the derelict gun platform. As Sealand, known at the time as HM Fort Roughs, was in international waters, Bates declared Sealand his own state. A British court ruled in 1968 that Sealand was outside British territorial waters, and in 1975, Roy Bates published a Constitution of the Principality of Sealand and began issuing passports. In 1999, Roy Bates gave way to his son, 'Prince Regent' Michael. Roy Bates died in 2012.

Listening for production

1 1 206 2 country 3 governmental 4 club

2 *Suggested answers*
1 a noun (You need a noun after a preposition.)
2 a countable noun (You need a countable noun after *how many*.)
3 a negative verb (*Do* seems to be functioning as an auxiliary in this sentence, as there does not seem to be a need for the emphatic use of *do*; the verb probably takes the dependent preposition *on*.)
4 a noun or noun phrase (*No* is used as a quantifier with nouns.)

3 1 the United Nations 2 common characteristics
3 not rely 4 single/one definition

Going further

Sample answer: The biggest difference is the source of sovereignty. In the constitutive school, sovereignty comes from the recognition of other sovereign states, while in the declarative school, it comes when a state meets a certain set of criteria.

Listening for meaning

1 2 dependable 3 unoriginal 4 nationalizing
5 territorial 6 Politicians

2 *Suggested answers*

1 constitute, constituencies, constituency, constituent, constituents, constituted, constitutes, constituting, constitution, constitutions, constitutional, constitutionally, constitutive, unconstitutional

2 create, created, creates, creating, creation, creations, creative, creatively, creativity, creator, creators, recreate, recreated, recreates, recreating

3 interpret, interpretation, interpretations, interpretative, interpreted, interpreting, interpretive, interprets, misinterpret, misinterpretation, misinterpretations, misinterpreted, misinterpreting, misinterprets, reinterpret, reinterpreted, reinterprets, reinterpreting, reinterpretation, reinterpretations

4 liberal, liberalise, liberalism, liberalisation, liberalised, liberalises, liberalising, liberalization, liberalize, liberalized, liberalizes, liberalizing, liberate, liberated, liberates, liberation, liberations, liberating, liberator, liberators, liberally, liberals

5 normal, abnormal, abnormally, normalisation, normalise, normalised, normalises, normalising, normalization, normalize, normalized, normalizes, normalizing, normality, normally

3 2 to enforce   3 not obtain   4 justify publishing
5 Is it legal   6 legislative   7 not relevant / irrelevant
8 established

Unit extension

1 1 b   2 c   3 d   4 a

2 1 weak   2 local   3 business/property
4 property/business   5 strong(er)   6 12th   7 king's law
8 similar case(s)   9 equal   10 centuries

3 1 central government is weak
2 the 12th century
3 Asserting their law
4 cases with new elements
5 precedent
6 hundreds of

4 2 difficulty   3 confused   4 localities   5 explanation
6 conclusion   7 likewise   8 incorrect   9 reasoning

5 1 give   2 ask   3 deal with   4 obey   5 assert   6 hear
7 give   8 set

Going further

C.	century
cntrol	control
crim'l	criminal
d'vlpmt	development
diff't	different
Eng.	English
gov't	government
jdg.	judge
prec.	precedent
re:	about
w/	with
x	for
=	equals

CONSOLIDATION 1

Topic focus

3 Television: viewing fees, spot, antenna, appliance, satellite
Newspapers: circulation, print, classified ad
Both: digital, journalist, subscribe, ad revenues

Vocabulary focus

1 daily, half, illegal, longer, onto, should, stations, struggle, view

2 1 play   2 break   3 behind   4 service   5 under

Practise your listening

1 1 c   2 a   3 a   4 b   5 c   6 b

2 1 advertising   2 1,408   3 Circulation
4 have been declining   5 a change in attitude

3 a sixteen point six
b twenty-three
c twenty-seven point five million
d forty-eight million, six hundred thousand
e fifty-six million, one/a hundred and eighty-two thousand, six hundred and thirty-five
f sixty-nine million, one/a hundred and twenty-five thousand, five hundred and seventy-three
g thirty-seven point eight five billion

4 1 c. = circa (Latin for *about*); yrs = years
2 lst = last; yr = year; approx. = approximately
3 ad. = advertising; rev. = revenue(s); % = per cent
4 ad. = advertising; lst = last; yr = year; $ = dollar(s)
5 ad. = advertising; rev. = revenue(s); lst = last; qrtr = quarter; approx. = approximately; $ = dollar(s)
6 % = percentage; x = for; approx. = approximately

5 1 e   2 d   3 a   4 g   5 c   6 b

6 69,125,573 = unique visits last month to newspaper websites

Going further

Suggested answer

According to Mr Wexler, the old business model for running a newspaper no longer works, and a new business model for running newspapers in the internet age has not been developed yet.

Unit extension

1 1 in the 1920s
2 It is designed to reach a large audience.
3 cost of duplicating materials declined + new technologies
4 the size of the audience of the Internet
5 paying for the separate pieces, rather than buying the whole thing

2 *Suggested answers*
1 reach a large audience
2 cost of duplicating materials declined
3 new technologies
4 audience (of the Internet)
5 buy single article, not whole magazine, or download song, not whole CD

3 *Suggested answers*
1 What are the two conceptions we have of the word *television*?
2 How will television be able to 'coexist' with the Internet?
3 How much did a 30-second spot cost for the last episode of *Lost*?
4 Why do people usually keep their cable once they've signed up?
5 How many people will tune in to watch the World Cup final?

4 1 necessarily   2 gathering   3 conception   4 relationship
5 projection   6 problematic   7 laziness   8 presidential

UNIT 4

Topic focus

3 *Suggested answers*
Natural: climate change, drug-resistant bacteria, earthquake, epidemic, extinction, landslide
Man-made: bio-tech disaster, computer overlords, nuclear accident
Space: alien attack, asteroid strike, supernova

Vocabulary focus

1 Space: ~ colony, ~ exploration, outer ~, ~ flight, deep ~
Disaster: avert ~, utter ~, natural ~, a recipe for ~,
on the brink of ~

3 1 b   2 c   3 It accelerates particles.   4 b   5 became/went
6 one-in-three

Practise your listening

1 1 no   2 732,600   3 ten million   4 on fire   5 no
6 black hole(s)   7 trillion

2 1 noted   2 galactic   3 (electrical) power grids   4 land
5 (advance) warning   6 flood   7 sucked (into)
8 likelihood

3 1 how probable   2 any undeniable   3 and by that
4 up to 716   5 calculate the probabilities   6 Not given
7 under the right

Language focus

1 1 also known as   2 British Broadcasting Corporation
3 European Union   4 frequently asked questions
5 Master of Business Administration   6 on the other hand

2 1 c   2 e   3 b   4 a   5 d

3 1 capt.   2 ex.   3 gov./gov't   4 inc.   5 km   6 syst'c

4 1 AD   2 LAT   3 ORIG   4 FWKO   5 ANZAC
6 HUD   7 YWHA   8 REM   9 MJur   10 ROTFL

5 1 before   2 I have questions about this information.
3 number   4 three times   5 causes / leads to / if … then
6 important

6 The two notes which do **not** represent information
mentioned in the extract are 3 and 6.

7 *Suggested answers*
1 Twenty million people were killed by the Spanish Flu in
1918.
2 The 'Black Death' was the name for the bubonic plague,
which killed roughly one-third of all Europeans.
4 Humans still face risks today from germs, for example
AIDS and Ebola, as well as other diseases.
5 When too many antibiotics are used, germs can develop
a resistance, as has happened with diseases like cholera
and tuberculosis.
7 There are around 30 different staph bacteria. Most are
harmless, but some can be very dangerous. Staph
bacteria are becoming more resistant to antibiotics.
8 Many mammals in the western hemisphere became
extinct around 12,000 years ago. Did they become
extinct because of disease?

Listening for production

1 1 a   2 c   3 a   4 c   5 The first word begins with a vowel,
and one of the words must be a noun.

2 1 the most probable   2 the 14th century   3 to have killed
4 the upper hand   5 ongoing threat

4 1 roughly 16 million   2 lasted until June
3 Globally, the death rate   4 Matters were made
5 most at risk of   6 majority of military deaths
7 lowered life expectancy   8 not belong solely to
9 flu's genetic sequence   10 if it makes

Listening for meaning

1 1 article   2 verb (*The British National Corpus does not
distinguish between auxiliary verbs and regular verbs.*)
3 preposition   4 conjunction   5 article   6 preposition
7 infinitive marker   8 verb (*see 2*)   9 pronoun
10 preposition   11 preposition   12 pronoun
13 conjunction   14 pronoun   15 pronoun

2 prep = preposition; v = verb; adv = adverb;
det = determiner; conj = conjunction; pron = pronoun;
poss = possessive

3 The actual words are:
16 on   17 with   18 do   19 at   20 by   21 not   22 this
23 but   24 from   25 they   26 his   27 that   28 she
29 or   30 which

4 But, what, would, if, our, into, with, a, Few, the, of, this,
but, do, that, there, are, in, the, and, are, the, of

6 *Few* scientists …
… *do* estimate …
… dead stars *are* …

7 1 every   2 a   3 but   4 some   5 do   6 those   7 than
8 Some   9 that   10 there   11 may   12 in

10 1 of the   2 itself   3 out of the   4 throughout   5 Given
6 one of these   7 If it   8 which could

Unit extension

1 Dr = Doctor
tchs = teaches
AKA = also known as
% = percentage
spcies = species
extnct = extinct
x75% = for 75%
E. = Earth
w/in = within
w/out spcl equip. = without special equipment
E'sytm = Ecosystem
rlt'ships b'twn = relationships between
gvn = given
Liv'g = Living
extnct. = extinction
# spcies extnct = number of species becoming extinct
r'frst = rainforest
yr = year
2 = to
trpcl r'frst collap. cld → = tropical rainforest collapse
could lead to
x humns = for humans
Mgntc. = Magnetic
revers. = reversal
(N↔S) = north goes south, south goes north
radiat. = radiation
s'brnd = sunburned
lst revers. = last reversal
Part. acc. = particle accelerator
Loc: Genv. + L. Isl. = located in Geneva and on Long
Island
NYC = New York City
AKA = also known as

2 1 Earth Science 312   2 Armageddon   3 99   4 20 minutes
5 all living organisms   6 25,000   7 780,000 years
8 100 kilometres east   9 black hole   10 strange matter

Going further

Suggested answers
1 ES312   2 Armgddn   3 –   4 20 min./mins
5 all lvg orgsms   6 –   7 780k yrs   8 100km E.   9 blk hle
10 str. mttr

UNIT 5

Vocabulary focus

1 a 4   b –   c 5   d 8   e 11   f 3   g 7   h 9   i 1   j 6   k 2
l 10

2 *Sample answer:* b (blame) = give responsibility for
something bad happening

3 1 outcome   2 no way   3 dissatisfaction/displeasure
4 standing   5 blameless   6 approach   7 insightful
8 turn out

Practise your listening

1 a, c, e

2 a Student A

    1 104   **2** to manage/limit   **3** careful
    4 worst-case scenario   **5** auto mechanics
    6 more accurately

  Student B

    1 3.6   **2** avoid bad outcomes   **3** Virginia
    4 Positive Psychology   **5** low self-esteem   **6** risk

 b **1** 104   **2** 3.6   **3** Virginia   **4** Positive Psychology
    5 more careful   **6** the worst-case scenario
    7 high standing   **8** auto mechanics   **9** a better
    10 evaluating risk(s)

Going further

In Track 2.16:

… the two are not unrelated.

Fortunately, it's not impossible …

In notes for Exercise 2a:

… not always inappropriate …

Language focus

1

cause	concession	contrast	result
due to because of owing to since	be that as it may albeit regardless of still	but however on the other hand whereas	so consequently therefore the result is

2 **1** Reaching a logical conclusion
   2 Introducing the topic
   3 Listing
   4 Beginning a new section
   5 Summarizing the talk
   6 Adding
   7 Returning to a topic
   8 Ending a section

3 *Sample answers*
   1 Reaching a logical conclusion
     As a consequence, …
   2 Introducing the topic
     My topic today is …
   3 Listing
     To begin with, …
     Last but not least, …
   4 Beginning a new section
     What I'd like to look at next is …
   5 Summarizing the talk
     To conclude, we have seen that …
   6 Adding
     Moreover, …
   7 Returning to a topic
     Anyway, where was I? Oh yes …
   8 Ending a section
     And that's all I want to say about …

4 **1** Because of the losses in the Central Asian markets
   2 That he has only been a lawyer for two years
   3 To attend court sessions
   4 Exports are calculated on their actual value, while tariffs are included in the calculation of imports.
   5 At a certain point, the cost of adding extra storage space will be higher than the benefit of adding it.
   6 That he had promised that the firm would not cut health benefits for at least five years
   7 Because of a 37% increase in the number of applications to Faber College

8 What's more (*Adding*); Thus (*Reaching a logical conclusion*)

5 although, and so, be that as it may, nevertheless, on the other hand, owing to, still, the result of that is, while

Going further

The two signals that were not used are *in spite of* and *regardless*.

6 **1** Lawyers are trained to think about risk, so they tend to look for the worst-case scenario.
   2 In spite of his pessimistic personality, Antonio is known as 'the happy lawyer'. / Antonio is known as 'the happy lawyer' in spite of his pessimistic personality.
   3 Whereas optimists generally do better at university than pessimists, this is not true of law students. / Optimists generally do better at university than pessimists, whereas this is not true of law students.

Listening for production

1 **1** Learned optimism
   2 *… is what I'd like to talk about tonight: …*

2 Defining 'optimism'

3 The 'three Ps'

4 *General topic*: The three Ps
   Key idea 1: Permanence; *information*: adversity temporary, not permanent
   Key idea 2: Pervasiveness; *information*: adversity unique, not a general problem
   Key idea 3: Personalization; *information*: pessimists blame themselves, optimists blame others

5 **1** f **2** a **3** g **4** b **5** c **6** d **7** e

7 These answers are optimistic:
   1 B **2** B **3** A **4** A **5** A **6** B **7** B **8** A

Going further

Personalization questions: 1, 2, 7

Pervasiveness questions: 5, 6

Permanence questions: 3, 4, 8

Listening for meaning

1 accurate, aspect, convinced, evaluating, outcome, research, scenario

2 **1** occupations **2** apparently **3** achievement **4** anticipating **5** specifically

3 **1** analyst **2** benefit **3** beneficial **4** conformity **5** conformist **6** minimalize **7** minimal **8** response **9** responder **10** responsive

4 **Across:** **2** constraint **8** evidence **11** final **12** anticipating **16** occupations **17** assure **19** odds **22** accuracy **23** issues **24** image **25** chart
   Down: **1** motivation **3** scenario **4** traditional **5** benefits **6** unique **7** goal **9** exports **10** dramatically **13** nevertheless **14** contrary **15** contradict **18** cycle **20** reject **21** quote

Unit extension

1 **a** 6 **b** 8 **c** 2 **d** 7 **e** 3 **f** 1 **g** 10 **h** 5 **i** 9 **j** 4

2 *Suggested answer*
   … why we aren't as happy as we could be and number these sentences in the order you hear them.

3 We are not very good at calculating probability.
   We are not good at estimating value.

4 **1** one in 13,983,816
   2 We are not very good at calculating probability.
   3 Obstacle
   4 … can do with the money.
   5 That we base our idea of value on what happened yesterday, not what something is worth today.

UNIT 6

Vocabulary focus

1 *Suggested answers*

positive	negative
affordable, classic, cutting-edge, exclusive, trendy, low-cost	cheap, common, stale, overrated, old-fashioned, generic

2 1 advertisement   2 campaign   3 consumers   4 image
5 launch   6 competitive advantage   7 motto   8 product
9 promotion   10 rebranding   11 sales   12 life cycle

3 1 consumers   2 motto   3 sales   4 Product; product
5 campaign   6 life cycle   7 competitive advantage
8 rebranding   9 image   10 launch

Going further

The two terms that were not used are *advertisement* and *promotion*.

Practise your listening

1 1 greatpointedarcher.com   2 T-shirts; mouse pads
3 schoolchildren   4 world war   5 breaking   6 has value

2 3 (Rebranding after a merger)

3 1 Both brands represented the same bar, but in the interests of global advertising, the parent company decided to rebrand **Marathon as Snickers**.
2 **Phillip Morris**, for example, changed its name to Altria because it did not want to be connected with tobacco any more.
3 In the case of the European Union, a decision to rebrand was taken in **1998** …
4 ~~Unfortunately,~~ the new motto – 'Unity in diversity' – was **included in the constitution**.
5 ~~It was discovered that an advertising agency had set up the campaign as a hoax.~~ No one knows who set up the campaign.
6 Before rebranding, it is important to remember that the old brand **still** has value.

Language focus

1 1 For what it's worth, …
2 If I could draw your attention to …   3 By the way, …
4 After all, …   5 Or rather …   6 As for …
7 Whereas …   8 To cut a long story short, …

2 1 in general   2 that is   3 As we've already seen
4 for instance
5 It goes without saying that; and this is really the key

3/4 2 To put it another way, … (category 3)
3 of course (category 7)   4 In fact, … (category 2)
5 such as (category 1)   6 Or rather, … (category 3)
7 The main thing (to remember) … (category 8)

5/6 1 basically (category 4)
2 Or rather (category 3)
3 such as (category 1)
4 To put it another way (category 3)
5 as I mentioned before (category 6)
6 broadly speaking (category 4)

7 1 I think it's worth (taking a few minutes to …)
2 But anyway, (let's get back to the question …)
3 So, …
4 Well, …

Listening for production

1 Topic: brands
Key ideas: 1 brands' function   2 two anti-brand books
3 brands' history

3 1 to identify   2 mid-1800s   3 industrialization   4 2000
5 globalization   6 *The Hidden Persuaders*   7 words
8 images

Listening for meaning

1 1 c   2 a   3 c   4 a   5 d   6 b   7 c   8 a

2 1 tried very hard to achieve something
2 an answer that covers a wide range of possible situations
3 have a relationship that has lasted a long time
4 a word that is considered 'bad', that you shouldn't use

Unit extension

1 1 There was no more 'shop owner' who knew your tastes and requirements and no one particular person that you knew was responsible for choosing the goods for sale.
2 Consistency
3 1,500
4 Marketing promotions
5 That other brands also offer consistency
6 The relationship consumers have with the brands they use
7 To expand on the idea that companies started focusing on building brands, not making products (also to give an example of outsourcing)
8 People want to know that they are spending their money well.

3 Organization B better represents the talk.

5 *Sample answer*
In her talk, Margaret Lee raises the question of why brands exist. Ms Lee suggests that one reason for brands is that they allow producers to distinguish their products as the marketplace has become more crowded. She points out that the expansion of distribution networks in the mid-19th century, due to industrialization and the development of longer-distance transport networks, increased the number of goods available to consumers. She also stresses that being able to distinguish a particular brand was good for consumers. A particular brand of soup, for example, offered them a level of quality and consistency in that crowded marketplace. The brand name gave consumers confidence that the can of soup they bought in the spring would taste the same as the can of soup they had bought in the winter. As the personalized relationships consumers had previously enjoyed with shop owners and artisans gave way to the spread of industrialization, this consistency became more important.

At the same time, Ms Lee also looks at why many people have a negative image of brands. She points out that even in the 1950s, consumers were unhappy with the idea that they were being manipulated into buying certain brands. A book from the era, *The Hidden Persuaders*, brought into the public arena the idea of subliminal advertising – the idea that advertisers were incorporating into their advertisements images and words targeted at the audience's subconscious.

She gives other reasons for the decline in brands' popularity. Brands face many more competitors than they did in the 19th century, and most of those competitors have products of similar quality. She also says that companies became more concerned with marketing their brands than with producing their products. This has led to the view that companies do not really make their own products any more. She concludes, however, that brands still have a role to play in the marketplace, and that they can still signal to people that they are spending their money effectively. (327 words)

CONSOLIDATION 2

Topic focus

1 *Suggested answers*
Syntax: object, preposition, pronoun, subject, tense, verb
Vocabulary: base word, gender, preposition, suffix
Pronunciation: consonant, stress, syllable

Vocabulary focus

1 1 h 2 j 3 e 4 a 5 k 6 g 7 i 8 l 9 b 10 c 11 d
12 f

2 1 point out 2 caveat 3 attribute 4 meticulously
5 one-off 6 reference 7 struck a chord 8 universal

Going further

The words/phrases that were not used are: *to turn out, to revitalize, commonality* and *inanimate*.

Practise your listening

1 a, c, e

2 1 Any two from: tenses; gender or another classification system; how the language identifies roles in a sentence
2 Any two from: structure; subjects; verbs; objects
3 Any two from: vowels; consonants; syllables; stress
4 Elements that are added to a base word, like when we take the verb *teach* and we add –*er* to make *teacher*.
5 *Suggested answer:* If a language has one element, then it will have another.
6 We all have the same brains and we all learn our mother tongue in more or less the same way.

3 *Sample answer*
One category of language universal is 'absolute universals'. Absolute universals are elements shared by every language. In syntax, linguists point to the fact that all languages have elements in sentences that function as subjects, verbs or objects as an example of an absolute universal. Other examples include the fact that certain elements of pronunciation – consonants, vowels and syllables, for example – are found in every language. Elements of vocabulary, too, seem to be universal. For instance, every language seems to have pronouns.
The other category of universal is known 'implicational universals'. 'Implicational' in this context means something like 'conditional'. If a language has one element, then it will have another. For example, not every language uses affixes, which are pieces added to a base word (English uses two types of affix: prefixes and suffixes), but there are some languages that use only suffixes. In these languages, you will find **post**positions (for example *Cambridge to*) rather than the prepositions found in English (*to Cambridge*).

Going further

2 masculine **3** syllables **4** object **5** consonant(s) **6** suffix
7 preposition(s) **8** pattern **9** vowel(s) **10** feature

Unit extension

2 1 also 2 so 3 in other words
4 It goes without saying that … 5 after all 6 even if
7 but 8 indeed 9 On the other hand, … 10 and
11 such as 12 As I mentioned before, …

3 1 such as 2 Indeed 3 It goes without saying that
4 but 5 even if 6 after all 7 also 8 On the other hand
9 And 10 So

4 1 has no more 2 as to why 3 The process of
4 over time, switches 5 as it's 6 community assimilate
7 high on the 8 conduct business 9 an endangered
10 open to debate

5 abbreviation	meaning/reference
Def.	definition
Lang.	language
c'not	cannot
Scient.	scientific
devlp'd	developed
AKA	also known as
LD	linguistic determinism
lang.	language
spkrs	speakers
Eng.	English
w/	with
W-S	Whorf-Sapir hypothesis
W's	Whorf's
NYC!	New York City (surprising information)
Lang. = info. mgmt (mostly)	Language is primarily concerned with information management.
info.	information
attn	attention
ex.	example
Fr.	French
Fr. v. Germ. v. Span.	French versus German versus Spanish
masc./fem.	masculine and feminine (genders)

6 1 talk about 2 1940s 3 Whorf-Sapir hypothesis
4 don't see time (in) 5 one Hopi speaker
6 Weak linguistic determinism 7 know the other person
8 *bridge*

8 The words *flow* and *linguistics* are not part of the AWL.

Academic Word List exercises

Unit 1

1 aspect 2 commit 3 consequences 4 assumptions
5 errors 6 wise 7 conclusion 8 requires 9 communicate
10 tasks 11 Finally 12 valuable

Going further
wise and *valuable* are not on the AWL.

Unit 2

1 designed 2 promoters 3 security 4 remove
5 projected 6 albeit 7 founders 8 release 9 Nonetheless
10 decade 11 percentage 12 distribution

Unit 3

1 d 2 a 3 b 4 a 5 b 6 c 7 a 8 c 9 c 10 b 11 d
12 b

Unit 4

1 1 somewhat 2 Despite 3 whereas 4 Nevertheless
2 1 approximately 2 communications 3 precision
4 range 5 range 6 area 7 so-called 8 impact
9 significant 10 odds 11 remove 12 theoretically
The words *option* and *scope* are not used. Gaps 4 and 5 contain an AWL word not in the box.

Unit 5

1 innovations 2 simulate 3 volunteers 4 accurate
5 affect 6 intense 7 uncontroversial 8 reject 9 reside
10 Dramatizing 11 adaptation 12 resourceful

Unit 6

1 participate 2 image 3 interactions 4 interact 5 tape